Endorsements

What a captivating read! Under God, Patrick Johnstone, through his tireless traveling, speaking, and creation of *Operation World*, has stimulated tens of thousands (that's no exaggeration) of believers around the world to pray more intelligently for the advance of the gospel in every country and every corner of the globe. We are deeply indebted to him. It is wonderful to read his life story and to feel something of the infectious spirit with which God has endowed this man. His material continues to be the surest means of informing the global church and any individual believer of how to pray for God's work in every nation under the sun. I couldn't put the book down. Read and be captivated yourself!

Dr. Lindsay Brown
General Secretary, IFES (1991–2007)
International Director, Lausanne Movement (2008–2017)

Operation World has been a force in God's hands for over six decades, stimulating passionate prayer and disciple-making among least-reached peoples. *God's World to Win* now gives us the back story. Patrick Johnstone shares his journey with compelling authenticity and demonstrates how a humble vision born in Africa has been used by God to mobilize millions across continents. His story has left me awed at what Jesus can do through a surrendered life. May his legacy inspire curious minds, informed intercession, and global teamwork for God's glory among the nations!

Dean Carlson, DMin
President, One Challenge
International Liaison, Movement for African National Initiatives

Operation World was like a spark that stirred up the hearts of believers towards believing that the Great Commission was doable. *God's World to Win* helps us to recognize the "hands" behind the scenes orchestrating the impact of *Operation World* right from that "spark," the fanning into the flame, the fueling and the controlling of the spread. Starting from the "finger of the Lord of the Harvest," the heart of the obedient servant of the Lord, the encouragement and involvement of several other servants of the Lord, and the hearts that caught the fire and started engaging in focused prayer and strategic engagement among the neediest sections of the Great Commission.

Reuben Ezemadu
International Director, Christian Missionary Foundation
Continental Coordinator, Movement for African National Initiatives

This fascinating story behind the book that has helped millions of Christians to pray meaningfully for the world also doubles as an inspiring autobiography of Patrick Johnstone. Reading this, we can glean many instructive principles on the Christian life, such as facing challenges and disagreements, involvement in mission, community living, and team dynamics. Along the way, we are introduced to some of the great people and movements that served to speed the work of reaching a lost world for Christ during a crucial period in the history of the church.

AJITH FERNANDO
Teaching Director, Youth for Christ, Sri Lanka
Author, *Discipling in a Multicultural World*

We simply cannot know, this side of eternity, the depth of the impact of Patrick Johnstone's ministry through *Operation World*. I welcomed him to the very first 24-7 prayer room in Chichester, England, before anyone knew that a global movement was being born. In that encounter, I discovered that this statesman of the church was a humble servant of Jesus. He didn't just talk about prayer; he was himself a man of prayer who carried a deep and compelling love for the nations and for the Lord Jesus Christ deep within his heart.

PETE GREIG
Founder, 24-7 Prayer International

Many people want to change the world, but relatively few have actually done so. Patrick Johnstone, through his creation and stewardship of *Operation World*, is someone who has. Patrick and his incredible team showed me what God is doing to draw people from every nation to himself, and how I could play a role in his mission. Read this honest and compelling account of how the Lord has used an ordinary man with an extraordinary vision. It will help you to see God's world with fresh eyes.

STAN GUTHRIE
Author, *Missions in the Third Millennium* and *Victorious: Corrie ten Boom and The Hiding Place*

This is a fascinating account of how God's people globally have been helped to pray great things for God's global purpose. This is the story of a historic change in how God's people pray. Left to ourselves, we pray for our own concerns. But there is tremendous dignity and joy knowing that God hears our voices along with many others. We have uttered prayers for distant lands and peoples, many times without knowing the names or places. But in the last few decades, Patrick Johnstone, along with his team, has given us specific names and numbers. This has enlarged our faith and brightened our hope: our God will fulfill what He has promised. Don't read this book to merely pray more. Read this to pray greater.

STEVEN HAWTHORNE
Lead Editor, *Perspectives on the World Christian Movement*

Don't miss this captivating story highlighting the origin and impact of *Operation World* and the prolific life of its author. Both Patrick and this book chronicle and have contributed to the Spirit-led explosion of prayer movements, an influx of new missionaries from Asia, Africa, and Latin America, and the harvest among previously unreached peoples over the last seventy years. In 1975, George Verwer, the late founder of Operation Mobilization, sent me an early edition of the book while my family and I were serving on OM's first ship, the M.V. *Logos*. We devoured it. Four years later, Patrick and Jill, accompanied by their three children, joined our international ministry team as we conducted the first *Operation World* Conferences and sold thousands of *Operation World* books in over a dozen Asian port cities.

DAVE HICKS
Director, OM Ship Logos
OM North America Area Coordinator, Bethany International
President, AlongsideASIA

I have had the great privilege of serving, and serving with, Patrick Johnstone over more than a decade of shared adventures in seeing the Lord multiply his church around the world. Whether in my role as a young tech/data entrepreneur or later as a behind-the-scenes advisor to leaders, Patrick has always been to me a gentle, servant-hearted example of godly maturity and excellence in action. Now, with *God's World to Win*, I have been delighted to see the personal roots that undergird Patrick's life. You too will be blessed by seeing God's great love in action in this amazing story of a life on adventure with God. Not perfect—many lessons learned every step of the way! Not "privileged"—Patrick had to learn great discipline and endurance to get through each battle.

PETE HOLZMANN
Founder/Exec Director, The International Christian Technologists' Association (ICTA)

As a fellow global researcher, I'm so pleased to follow Patrick's engaging story of a lifetime commitment to both faith and research. He poignantly recalls the pain, disappointments, and sacrifices, punctuated by the victories and rewards in which so many Christians around the world were impacted by both his life and *Operation World*. A must-read for Christians of all kinds: God's world expertly portrayed, and a life well lived!

TODD M. JOHNSON, PhD
Eva B. and Paul E. Toms Distinguished Professor of Mission and
Global Christianity, Gordon-Conwell Theological Seminary

In content, style, and format, *Operation World* has been a standard to which I aspire and compare all my own research and analysis. As a leader and elder in research, Patrick himself has been one of the principal formative influences on my life: kind, generous, clarifying, gently critiquing, encouraging. We all want to be Patrick when we grow up. *God's World to Win*—his story, and the story of *Operation World*—is one of the books I have been waiting eagerly to read, just to hear his voice in print once more.

JUSTIN LONG
Missionary researcher with Beyond
Editor, Weekly Roundup

Patrick introduced me to mission information, first through several editions of *Operation World* and then through the pages of *The Church Is Bigger Than You Think*. So, what a delight it was that in my first mission project, he was on hand to mentor me in person. As God led me to pray for and develop mission information work as a profession, I realized that, as with any other godly endeavor, we need history. *Operation World* is central to our history. I gave Patrick a few hints, which he acknowledged, but he remained busy with other important things. Finally, I got down on my knees in front of him and begged him to write this book. I am not disappointed. Thank you, Patrick.

CHRIS MAYNARD
Founder Member, Community of Mission Information Workers

We are honored to endorse Patrick's new book, which reflects his faithful and Spirit-led ministry in Christ. His commitment to the gospel, demonstrated through research and intercessory prayer, has deeply blessed the global church. It is God's strategy to advance his Kingdom. *Operation World* has played a remarkable role in missions. When Mission Korea launched in 1988, campus prayer meetings began using the book, sparking a nationwide mission movement. One mission agency even uses it for a 24-hour, 365-day prayer relay. The 1986 edition inspired me (KyungNam) to start campus mission prayer. KyoungA led prayer meetings with insights from the book and consistently recommended it to mission candidates and churches. The book helped us decide to choose a mission field where the Gospel had not yet been proclaimed. We thank God who called Patrick and did His marvelous work through him. We pray God will continue to use *Operation World* under Jason Mandryk's leadership—for His glory.

KyungNam Park, MD, and **KyoungA Park**, MD
International Directors, WEC International

Patrick Johnstone is a dear friend from the decade of the 1990s when we both had the great joy and honor of being selected to co-lead the Unreached Peoples Track for the AD2000 and Beyond Movement, he as chairman and I as coordinator. Those years, as Patrick wrote in his recent message to me, were "the greatest ingathering into God's Kingdom ever," a time of fruitful harvest, with large numbers coming to Christ as the worldwide body of Christ was challenged to engage in an all-out effort in united prayer and mission engagement. Our goal was the remaining *panta ta ethne* of Matthew 28:19 and 24:14, the thousands of people groups still needing a witness to Jesus through the ignition of endlessly replicating movements of his followers, to carry the gospel through their unique cultures, languages, and worldviews so it could be understood and received with heartfelt faith. During those years, hundreds of interdenominational networks were formed to reach these people groups. Patrick's wide-ranging knowledge of global missions and the status of these unreached people groups, displayed in successive editions of *Operation World* and in our AD 2000 consultations, was always deeply appreciated by me and our other colleagues. You will be greatly encouraged and blessed to read *God's World to Win* with its many precious lessons from his long life and extraordinary service for the Lord of the harvest.

John Robb
Coordinator, Unreached Peoples Task Force

Operation World has helped millions of Christians expand their daily prayers from personal and local concerns to a global perspective on the church. Having translated several editions into German, I could see how it shaped and changed the landscape for those engaged in world mission, even opening a new dimension for Christians at large in the German speaking countries. Millions have learned that the world is made up not just of UN member states, but of a vast number of diverse ethnic groups, languages, and social situations, all loved by God alike. I believe that it helped millions to better understand John's vision in the book of Revelation of an innumerable multitude from all nations, tribes, peoples and languages worshipping the Lamb together. The time had come to write the history of *Operation World* as a vital element of world mission and world history over the last fifty years.

THOMAS SCHIRRMACHER
President, International Institute for Religious Freedom
Former Secretary General, World Evangelical Alliance
Archbishop of the Confessing Anglican Church
Professor of World Mission

In *God's World to Win*, Patrick Johnstone recounts the remarkable history of the life-impacting book *Operation World*. *Operation World* has radically changed the direction of many lives, including my own. I first encountered *Operation World* in a college prayer group. Praying through it powerfully opened my eyes to a global picture of Christianity and the spiritual needs of each country in the world. *God's World to Win* encourages and challenges as it traces the humble beginnings of *Operation World* and its growth to become one of the most significant and impactful books in Christian missions. *God's World to Win* is a powerful reminder of the Lord's faithfulness in the past and the promise that one day there will be some from every tribe, tongue, nation, and people worshipping the Lamb. Thank you, Patrick, for the gift of *God's World to Win* to the global Church.

DAN SCRIBNER
Operations Director, Joshua Project

This is more than the story of a book that changed the world. It is a deeply personal account of the man behind the book and the God behind that man. The book combines both an inspiring account of the global work of God with the humility and honesty of the man being transformed and used by God. As I read the book, my heart was stirred afresh in awe and admiration of Jesus, seeing how He used one faithful man, Patrick Johnstone, and one book, *Operation World*, to impact countless lives so deeply for missions and so many nations for Christ.

Louis Sutton
International Director (2011–2022), WEC International

With every year I've used *Operation World* as a prayer guide for global evangelization, my respect and appreciation for Patrick Johnstone climbs higher. This beloved brother has constantly stoked his mission-minded passion to see Christ's gospel permeate some of the darkest places on the globe. Patrick's story alone would make his new work *God's World to Win* a must-read. But it's true value lies in the fascinating stories of humble missionaries, world-acclaimed scholars, and ordinary people that God wove together to advance his Kingdom wherever there›s no hope. Pick up *God's World to Win*, turn the page and be inspired to share Christ's good news in *your* world.

Joni Eareckson Tada
Joni and Friends International Disability Center

Patrick Johnstone has left an indelible mark on global missions through his vision, scholarship, and faith. His book *God's World to Win* is not merely a history of *Operation World*—it is a testimony to how one man's obedience to God has shaped generations of believers. I experienced this firsthand as a young participant in the Doulos Intensive Training program, where we were required to pray through every country in *Operation World*. That discipline transformed my prayer life and radically expanded my worldview. Later, in 2001, I had the privilege of meeting Patrick aboard the *LOGOS II* in London, where, as ship director, I hosted the launch of a revised edition of *Operation World*. I was thrilled to honor the very man whose work had inspired me years earlier. Patrick's life and writings continue to call us to faith, humility, and passionate prayer for the nations.

Lawrence Tong, PhD
International Director, Operation Mobilisation

GOD'S WORLD TO WIN

The Story of Operation World

Patrick Johnstone
with Paul Hattaway

visit us at missionbooks.org

God's World to Win: The Story of Operation World
© 2026 by Patrick Johnstone. All Rights Reserved.

No part of this book may be reproduced, stored in a retrieval system, or transmitted in any form or by any means—electronic, mechanical, photocopy, recording, or otherwise—without prior written permission from the publisher, except brief quotations used in connection with reviews. This manuscript may not be entered into or used to train any AI system without the publisher's written consent (permissions@wclbooks.com). For corrections, email editor@wclbooks.com.

William Carey Publishing (WCP) publishes resources to shape and advance the missiological conversation in the world. We publish a broad range of thought-provoking books and do not necessarily endorse all opinions set forth here or in works referenced within this book.

The URLs included in this book are provided for personal use only and are current as of the date of publication, but the publisher disclaims any obligation to update them after publication.

Scriptures are taken from the Holy Bible, New International Version®, NIV®. Copyright © 1973, 1978, 1984, 2011 by Biblica, Inc.™ Used by permission of Zondervan. All rights reserved worldwide. www.zondervan.com. The "NIV" and "New International Version" are trademarks registered in the United States Patent and Trademark Office by Biblica, Inc.™

Published by William Carey Publishing
10 W. Dry Creek Cir
Littleton, CO 80120 | www.missionbooks.org

William Carey Publishing is a ministry of Frontier Ventures
Pasadena, CA | www.frontierventures.org

Cover and Interior Designer: Mike Riester

ISBNs: 978-1-64508-683-3 (paperback)
    978-1-64508-685-7 (epub)

Printed Worldwide
30 29 28 27 26   1 2 3 4 5   IN

Library of Congress Control Number: on file

CONTENTS

A Word from Jason Mandryk		xiii
Foreword by Paul Hattaway		xvii
1	The Early Years	1
2	Meeting My Creator	7
3	Preparing for Service	11
4	Hitting the Ground Running—Apartheid, Witchcraft, and Revival	15
5	Jill	23
6	Learning to Walk in the Spirit	27
7	1964—The First *Operation World*	31
8	Rhodesia	37
9	The Long Path to Marriage	45
10	Married Life and Ministry	53
11	1974—*Operation World 2*	61
12	Banishment	69
13	1978—*Operation World 3*	75
14	Out of Africa	81
15	Life on the Ocean Waves	89
16	Burnout	97
17	A Research Team	105
18	A Mega-Shift at WEC	111
19	1986—*Operation World 4*	119
20	The Decade of Harvest	125
21	The Lord Calls Jill Home	131
22	A Church for Every People by the Year 2000	137

23	1993—*Operation World 5*	147
24	Robyn	153
25	The Tour from Hell	159
26	*The Church Is Bigger than You Think*	165
27	2001—*Operation World 6*	171
28	Handover Time	177
29	*The Future of the Global Church*	185
30	Life Lessons	193
31	A World Still to Win	197

About the Authors   203

A Word from Jason Mandryk

On a frigid and otherwise unremarkable winter day in Manitoba, my life took a major unanticipated turn. I was a second-year seminary student with a sense of calling to world mission that was clear in conviction but frustratingly vague in scope. Much effort had been spent learning about different agencies, countries, peoples, and ministries, but I still had no clarity about where the Lord was sending *me*. Enter one Patrick Johnstone, whose firehose model of public speaking involved a five-centimeter stack of overhead transparencies (yes, I am that old) and a breathless yet sustained tempo of impartation. Patrick wove together passages and principles from Scripture, anecdotes from the mission field and his own life, and data visualizations in the form of maps, charts, and graphs into a tapestry that brought a richness and depth to the Great Commission I had never before encountered. He delivered this message with warmth and humor, passion and authority. During that seminar, I felt the Lord speaking to me with more clarity than I had ever experienced before or since: "What Patrick is doing is what I am calling you to do."

Fourteen months later, I was in England, enthusiastic but largely unprepared for what would come next. An initial two-year commitment stretched into twenty-five years. None of these years would have happened had Patrick not said yes to traversing the notoriously and bitterly cold Canadian Prairies on a speaking tour in the middle of winter. The years certainly would not have extended beyond the first two had Patrick not been the man of great giftedness, godliness, and graciousness that I have come to know.

As I grew to know Patrick as a person, my admiration for him only deepened. Indulge me as I share a few of the many reasons why:

- Patrick is a minister of the gospel before he is a researcher. While he does get excited by data, his heart primarily longs for people to encounter the love and person of Jesus. Furthermore, he is a child of God who adores his heavenly "Abba" even before he is a minister of the gospel.

- He is a disciple-maker, mentoring people in their spiritual lives and training them in research methods. I was challenged and stretched in both areas—he has played the role of Paul to many Timothys throughout his life of ministry. In virtually all our testimonies, Patrick would push us out of the nest before we fledglings thought we were ready—only for us to discover that he had prepared us to fly well!

- He is a model of ingenuity. Who could imagine compiling a global prayer guide from the back of a van while doing itinerant evangelism in the slums of Africa, under apartheid regimes, with postal sanctions imposed, in the 1960s? Yet Patrick found solutions. "Ingenious" is an entirely appropriate word for someone who devised methods for enumerating evangelicals, developing taxonomies of people groups, and estimating the progress of global mission—all with limited time, budget, and technology!

- Finally, he is a model of transparency and spirituality, which I aspire to. Patrick is open about his own flaws and areas for growth. There is no "private" Patrick as an alter ego to the well-known author and speaker. Virtually every conversation of substance I've had with him ended with him suggesting that we pray and leading us in prayer.

The story of Operation World is a story of *convergence*. This word has become a defining term for how we at Operation World see God's kingdom unfolding in our age. In the past generation, we have witnessed the remarkable growth of a global movement of prayer—or rather, of countless interconnected movements. At the same time, with the impetus of people like Patrick, David

Barrett, and others, we have seen the flourishing of Christian research and information. Third, the global mission movement has become truly polycentric, emerging from the restricting chrysalis of Western colonialism. The great breakthroughs are now coming as these three movements converge, interact, and multiply each other's impact. Such breakthroughs are worth sharing about and praying for. And so, our work continues.

So much has changed in the world since Patrick's first *Operation World* sixty years ago. So much has changed since *my* first *Operation World* twenty-four years ago! The state of the global church and the understanding of mission have profoundly shifted. Technological revolutions have utterly disrupted and transformed not only how we do research but also how we engage with information. We now maintain an Operation World mobile app and website even as we work on publishing a new edition of the book. Our team is working on a first draft even as I write this—we are picking up pace, but with over two hundred countries to cover, it is no small task! Composition is proving to be a monumental challenge as world events race past us at breakneck speed, while our societies, churches, and devotional lives are completely rewired in record time. The team needs an impossible degree of wisdom and discernment to complete a global guide on praying for every nation. Thankfully, the Lord of the harvest is also the God of the impossible.

Foreword

by Paul Hattaway

I am deeply honored to help Patrick Johnstone write *God's World to Win: The Story of Operation World*. People may experience several key moments that prove pivotal to the direction of their lives. For me, my first contact with Patrick and his ministry took place on a Monday morning in October 1987. The previous evening, I attended my first church meeting, where I heard the gospel for the first time. I asked God to forgive my sins, and I surrendered my life to Jesus.

My friend Darren watched in shock as I walked forward to publicly commit my life to Christ. Little more than twelve hours after my life-changing conversion, he drove me to a Christian bookstore and bought two books for me—a study Bible and *Operation World* by Patrick Johnstone.

Over the following weeks and months, I devoured the Scriptures and, through the influence of *Operation World*, gained clarity about how my life could count for the kingdom of God. Within six months, I found myself in China on a six-week mission trip to deliver Bibles to persecuted house church believers. Despite being a new teenage believer with no support, money, or worldly prospects, it didn't feel right to go home at the scheduled time. By the grace of God, that initial six-week trip has grown into an ongoing 36-year adventure serving the Body of Christ throughout Asia.

My second contact with Patrick came a decade after my conversion when I found myself in a departure lounge at Los Angeles International Airport, waiting for a British Airways flight to Heathrow, London. After attending a conference at the US Center for World Mission, where Patrick was one of the main speakers, I was burning up with a fever and just wanted to get into my seat, wrap a blanket around my head, and hopefully sleep through the flight.

As I waited for the boarding call, I was surprised when Patrick came over and sat down next to me. Seeing that I was unwell, he disappeared and returned a few minutes later with some medicine from the airport pharmacy. He lovingly helped me take it, and during the flight, I was again shocked when the author of my favorite missions book came to my seat at the back of the plane to check on me and encourage me with stories about what God was doing around the world.

This incident, which he didn't remember when I mentioned it to him in preparation for this book, spoke volumes to me as Patrick—a best-selling author and renowned global missions statesman—modeled how a servant of God should humbly and graciously care for others.

A few more years passed before my third key interaction with the author of this book. By 1999, I had accumulated a large box of loose papers and printed photographs from my years of traveling in China. Despite the Chinese government claiming there are only 56 official ethnic groups in the country, I had documented and photographed nearly 500 distinct peoples. My dream was to produce a large, full-color book to aid the kingdom of God.

As the months passed, it felt like my dreams for the book were at a dead end. I was told that no publisher was interested in such a large and expensive project. Then one evening, while at home in northern Thailand, I thought I should call Patrick Johnstone in England to see if he had any advice for me.

As I shared my predicament with him, Patrick encouraged me not to give up hope, reassuring me that God had surely not enabled me to find and document so many new groups for the information to remain hidden. Then he asked, "Have you tried my friend Pieter Kwant? He is starting a new publishing company, and this could be a great first project for him."

"Pieter who?" I replied.

A few weeks later, I made my way to Carlisle near the Scottish border with the precious box of papers and photos tucked under my arm and spent an afternoon with Pieter and Elria Kwant. The rest is history. At the beginning of the new millennium, the full-color, 704-page *Operation China* was published, with Patrick writing the foreword.

Although our journeys with the Lord on different sides of the globe meant our communication has mostly been by email since then, I have continued to hold Patrick and his ministry in high esteem. It is a great privilege to assist him with this book, completing a circle in my life that God began decades ago.

When I reached out to various mission leaders to ask what Patrick Johnstone and *Operation World* meant to them, all spoke of the deep respect they hold for him and the signature book that will always be linked to his name.

The fact that Patrick's scholarship is lauded almost goes without saying—*Christianity Today* included *Operation World* in its list of the fifty most influential Evangelical books of all time—but it was the comments on Patrick's character that caught my attention. The respondents spoke warmly of his faith and integrity, with one mission leader describing him as the "quintessential British gentleman."

All spoke of how his life and ministry had powerfully impacted them. Dan Scribner of the Colorado-based Joshua Project, said, "Patrick is a delightful and brilliant man, yet very approachable and engaging. He is quick to share his knowledge, laughs easily, asks good questions, provides exceptional insights, and offers his opinion but is not overbearing. He has been a mentor and dear friend for over three decades."

Loren Muehlius, who has produced maps together with Patrick since the 1980s, offered this tribute: "He is one of my heroes in mission research and has always been a great person to work with. Patrick shows care for each of us who worked on a project with him, and he is humble and intelligent. He has a British sense of humor and will share what is on his mind, but in a respectful way if it's controversial."

Now in his mid-80s, Patrick's passion to see God's kingdom come to every part of the world and to all people groups is undiminished. His mind remains sharp, and his heart focused. Although his advancing years meant he had to give up playing tennis a few years ago, his competitive nature now finds an outlet in table tennis, leaving some youngsters at his local club feeling embarrassed after losing to a man more than sixty years their senior!

Patrick recently shared how his great love for maps—which began as a shared interest with his father—continues today. He plays a daily online game where the silhouette of a country is displayed, and competitors have six chances to name it. He seemed vexed when telling me that in the previous four hundred days, he had gotten two answers wrong, but "only because in both cases they gave the single 'main' island as representing the whole!"

As Patrick Johnstone approaches the final laps of his earthly ministry, it is my hope and prayer that *God's World to Win: The Story of Operation World* will encourage and enrich your faith, focusing you on what has been the consistent heartbeat of Patrick's ministry for six decades: the glory of God among the nations and an unquenched desire to see the light of the gospel shine into every unreached part of the world.

①

The Early Years

In writing *God's World to Win: The Story of Operation World*, my desire is to reveal what God has done in the nations and peoples of the world in recent years, as well as the contributions of many involved in producing successive editions of *Operation World*. This narrative also includes details of my own personal journey. I often see my life and the journey the Lord has led me on, which culminated in the production of *Operation World*, as a large, multi-layered onion. Some layers are genetic, others are part of my human heritage, and still others are distortions and lies I believed about myself that had to be exposed and dealt with in the light of God and his word.

In the seventeenth century, my forefathers migrated from the Scottish borderlands to Ireland. Later, in 1899, my grandfather and uncle relocated to England, where they worked as medical practitioners in Gloucestershire. In 1917, my grandmother tragically lost her life when an attending doctor unwittingly allowed her to bleed to death during a miscarriage. My grandfather never recovered from that devastating loss, and in the process, he became addicted to morphine. My father, Maxwell (better known as Peter), was just eleven at the time, but despite the ensuing tragic home situation, he graduated and continued the family tradition in medicine by becoming an anesthetist at St. Thomas' Hospital, opposite London's Houses of Parliament.

My dad loved his job and his circle of friends, but when his father asked him to return home in 1936 to help with the country practice, he gave up his happy social life and attractive salary in London. One other reason my grandfather requested his help was that he had been placed on a list of registered addicts and needed my father's assistance in the practice and to administer his morphine dose. The loyalty my dad displayed became a model for my life and shaped my character.

My wonderful mother, Trudy, grew up in the town of Sliedrecht in the Netherlands. Her childhood was also dominated by a major family tragedy: the break-up of her parents' marriage. Neither Trudy nor her brother fully recovered from that trauma, which created a passionate desire in my mother's heart to preserve the integrity and closeness of her family.

My parents first met at a ski resort in Sweden, where my father was part of a group of holidaying English doctors. They married in 1937, but my mother experienced immediate culture shock when, at the tender age of twenty, she took over the management of a large English household with five servants, two acres of gardens, and an attic filled with half a century's worth of items stored by the extended family. Then just a year after my birth, all connections with her family and homeland were cut with the German invasion and occupation of the Netherlands.

I was born a year later, just before the outbreak of the Second World War, having inflicted my dear mother with toxemia. She was warned not to have more children but proceeded to have five more—all of whom were delivered safely.

The war years were difficult for my parents, and my father's health deteriorated. To cope with the stress, he became a heavy smoker, fell into depression, and developed ulcers that required surgery to remove most of his stomach.

My siblings and I spent much of the war cooped up because our large home served not only as our residence, but also as a doctors' office for three practitioners. I developed a passion for mischievous behavior, such as when I opened the valve of the upstairs radiator to create a puddle on the floor to paddle in, which dripped down to the dining room table below. Although we often fought among ourselves, my brother, sisters, and I became close companions. We banded together to protect each other against perceived external threats, and our friendship has continued throughout our lives, despite being scattered around the globe as we forged different career paths. Notwithstanding the intensity of our competition and frequent arguments on the court, I gained a lifelong passion for playing tennis.

My carefree boyhood ended abruptly at the age of nine when I was sent to a boarding school. Later, I was sent to Malvern College, where C. S. Lewis had also attended for a time, although he hated it so much that his parents were persuaded to remove him early. I struggled with the harsh discipline and rigidity of the school. I was a late developer, with my voice finally breaking when I was sixteen. Until then, I stood just over five feet tall and could not compete equally with my peers. My sports were gymnastics, tennis, and shooting—none of which garnered respect from my classmates, and I was frequently bullied by frllow students. All this cultivated within me a deep sense of inadequacy and failure. My five years at Malvern were the unhappiest of my life. I didn't dare tell my parents of my struggles, however, as they had sacrificed much to enable their children to benefit from a private education.

I also struggled academically, though I managed to complete enough schoolwork to graduate. Around half a century later, I discovered that I suffer from something called Auditory Processing Disorder (APD), which is similar to dyslexia. It often irritated my teachers and others that I was unable to follow instructions. A key characteristic of APD is that the initial part of a person's spoken message gets jumbled between my ears and brain. Over the course of my life, my most common phrase has been, "What did you say?" My struggles are exacerbated when I cannot see a person's face, as I need to lip-read to help determine the meaning of what is being said. This explains my lifelong dread of using a phone, which some mission leaders may have found strange!

Over the years, I developed mechanisms to cope better with this developmental issue, but only recently did I realize that I was different from other people. In retrospect, I now understand how APD contributed to my early social struggles and marginalization. I wish I had known about my condition as a schoolboy, but like the many branches on the autism spectrum, nothing was known of such things at the time. My ability to learn only developed when I completely reformed my study methods. I began to write notes and categorize them with different color headings. I barely scraped through to pass one subject of three at the end of my secondary education while at Malvern, but later at university, my new study technique meant I had no problem with learning, and I even gained an honors degree in chemistry.

I left Malvern College in July 1957 with no clear idea of what I should do with my life. Before my exam results arrived in the mail, our family went on a holiday to one of our favorite beaches—Tintagel on the north Cornish coast. Tintagel is the site of an early medieval castle—purported to have once been the home of the legendary King Arthur—and overlooks a small cove. At the time, my father was still recuperating from major surgery, as the earlier operation to remove most of his stomach had not gone well. I made my way out into the cove, but not being a very good swimmer, I soon headed back to the shore. My father passed me as he swam out to the entrance of the cove wearing his snorkel. It was great to see my dad enjoying himself, but I remember feeling profoundly concerned about how much stamina he had so soon after his surgery.

When I reached the beach, I went to retrieve my towel, and as I looked down at my father's towel and watch, an inexplicable dread came over me—will I ever see him again? I dismissed the thought, but just a few minutes later, there was a cry that a swimmer was in trouble. In the distance, I could see my father floating lifelessly at the entrance to the cove. Two kind men retrieved his body. The glass of his snorkel was broken, so we surmised that he had grown tired, and a wave had smashed his face into a rock, causing him to drown.

This tragedy was life-changing for my entire family. Our parents had poured so much into our education that there was not much remaining of my father's wealth, and we were living in my mother's father-in-law's home. My mother was suddenly a 40-year-old widow with six children and in need of a new home. As the eldest son, I realized that I might have to become my family's chief breadwinner. My grief-stricken grandfather died a few months later, at which point the house and property were divided among my father's surviving siblings.

I struggled to come to grips with my father's passing and the instability it caused, but in the years that followed, I came to appreciate the time I had spent with him. He taught me how to play chess in the evenings, and we would often spend hours looking at an atlas and making discoveries together. These precious interactions with my dad gave me a great love for maps, which greatly impacted my later life and ministry. I treasure those memories.

2

Meeting My Creator

The period of grieving for my father was followed by a season of intense soul-searching for the meaning and purpose of life. Throughout my teenage years, I had given little thought to eternal issues, as my focus was preoccupied with surviving my hostile school environment. Often my father had asked me what I wanted to do with my life, but I dodged his questions because I simply didn't know.

My father's death was a horrendous wake-up call, yet I had no answers to the key questions of life. Deep down, I felt a gnawing spiritual emptiness. I didn't know the purpose of my life, what happens when someone dies, or if there is an afterlife. Like most people in England at the time, I had been exposed to an Anglican expression of broad-church Christianity, so I was familiar with the general contents of the Bible but oblivious to my need for a personal relationship with the Lord Jesus Christ. As far as I was aware, none of my teachers was a committed Christian, and no one had ever confronted me with the need for a personal faith.

The course of my life dramatically altered in an extraordinary way when I was seventeen. At the time, I had been reading voraciously, devouring books and articles about the challenges of apartheid and the treatment of urban Africans in South Africa. One night, as I lay in bed, I believe God spoke directly to me, saying, "I want you to go for me to Africa!" This powerful revelation was difficult to explain to others, but it felt so real that I was overwhelmed by a mixture of wonder and panic.

Not knowing what to do next, I visited the school chaplain and asked him how I could "join the church." His response was not helpful; he warned me that I would not earn much money as a servant of God. He was unable to lead me to a personal meeting with the Lord Jesus. This frustrated me—I needed help but didn't know what I needed or how to find it. That special call from the Holy Spirit was placed on the shelf of my life, where I hoped to leave it until I could process it at a more appropriate time.

I realized the seriousness of my family's situation, with my mother now a single parent of six children with a limited income. Although I initially failed to obtain the results needed to attend university, I felt a strong responsibility as the eldest child to make another attempt to gain the grades needed to study chemistry—a subject that deeply interested me. The local Technical College in Gloucester covered the entire A-level course in one very intensive year. Now that I had devised a study method that worked well with my "disorder," I passed with ease, earned good grades that made a university place possible, and was even awarded a government grant to cover the cost of the degree course.

I was one of four candidates interviewed by Bristol University for the final place in their chemistry class for the upcoming school year. I was accepted, and it turned out to be orchestrated by the Lord, even though I was still not a committed Christian. Unbeknownst to me, Bristol University at that time was an institution with a particularly lively and strong Christian witness.

At the beginning of the second semester of my first year in 1959, I met Peter Marshall, who was a few years older than I. God used Peter to impact my life in a wonderful way. At the time he was studying for the Anglican ministry at what is now Trinity Theological College. He went on to serve the Lord in both youth ministry and pastoral work for many decades. After spending time with him, I realized he had what I was desperately searching for—a peace with God, an assurance of salvation, and confidence in God's guidance in his life.

Peter became a lifelong friend, and I will always be thankful for the influence he had in my life. Even as this book was being prepared for publication in 2024, Peter traveled from north Wales to spend time with me. I was speaking at my first mission conference since COVID-19, and it was emotional to see him again—Peter aged ninety and me eighty-five. We both have a lifetime of testimonies of God's loving goodness and mercy.

Previously, I thought I was already a Christian because God had spoken to me in that strange moment at Malvern, but my contact with real believers in Bristol showed that I needed to cross the line into a personal relationship with Jesus Christ. He needed to be in the driver's seat of my life, and my role was to love and obey him. One night, I waited until my agnostic roommate fell asleep, then I got out of bed, knelt, and gave myself to the Lord, asking him to take charge of my life. I began to read the Bible daily, and stimulated by fellowship with Peter and other Christians, I entered a new intimacy with God as my faith and knowledge grew.

Peter was a great discipler who urged me to get involved with outreach. I joined the Christian Union at the university, which had about three hundred members. Many became lifelong friends. I reveled in the fellowship, prayer meetings, Bible teaching, and social occasions. Peter also got me involved in student teams that ministered in churches and at summer camps.

At the beginning of the school year, I attended a local Anglican church, but as I matured in the Lord, I realized the preaching and theology were not compatible with the rich diet I was receiving from a series of superb preachers at the campus meetings. Peter also invited me to hear speakers at his Bible college, where both Alec Motyer and Jim Packer were lecturers. They later became known throughout the evangelical world as two of the foremost theologians of the twentieth century.

One day, a friend encouraged me to attend a special meeting where a missionary from Hudson Taylor's China Inland Mission (now Overseas Missionary Fellowship) was speaking. After the meeting, I bought the two volumes of Taylor's biography. They profoundly impacted me and made me determined never to settle for mediocrity in standards of faith and godliness should I ever become involved in missionary work.

Several years after my father's death, an old friend returned to our lives. Geoff Stebbing, who had become a family friend during the war, proposed to my mother, who then consulted each of us about how we felt. All six of us approved, so Geoff not only became a husband but also the stepfather of six children, although three of us had already completed school. Geoff and my mother enjoyed many happy years together.

Looking back, I can see how God's gracious hand helped me overcome those difficult years as he cleared a pathway for me to discover the purpose of my life.

Preparing for Service

After entering into a personal relationship with Jesus, I remembered what God had said to me at school about serving him. A few months later, a missionary, Glyn Davies, visited the university and spoke to about fifty students. When I arrived late to the meeting, the speaker was showing slides of Christian tent evangelism in the townships of South Africa. It felt like an electric shock surged through my body as God impressed upon my heart that this was his plan for me. This was my future! When I got home that evening, it felt like I was in a dream.

As I sat on my bed and asked God for confirmation that this intense feeling was more than just emotion, I knelt and opened my Bible. The page opened to this verse: "Ask me, and I will make the nations your inheritance, and the ends of the earth your possession" (Ps 2:8). To me, South Africa was the end of the earth. It was just the confirmation I had sought, and that Scripture became one of the great anchor points of my life in God's service—especially during times of doubt and discouragement.

Looking back more than sixty years later, I can say that God has indeed given me the nations—through writing about his kingdom and visiting many countries, where I have been privileged to encourage Christians to pray for and reach the unevangelized peoples of the world.

During my three years in Bristol, I had regular contact with the representatives of the Dorothea Mission, Glyn and Mary

Davies. I loved their company and got to know them well, reveling in their stories of ministry in Wales and Africa, and their heritage rooted in the Welsh Revival. When I shared that God had called me to Africa, a long and fruitful association began.

I was committed to completing an honors degree in chemistry, even though I knew I would eventually go to Africa when the time was right. Many wondered what use a science degree would be for the work ahead of me on the mission field, but I am so grateful for the stretching of my mind and the exposure to the world of research that my education provided. It equipped me with the tools I later needed to research *Operation World* and enabled me to process the mass of statistics that underpin the portrayal of the spiritual needs of the countries of the world. God never wastes any experience in our lives when we are fully committed to him!

As my university career drew to a close, I remained uncertain about what to do next. I was still less than three years old as a Christian, and I needed to prove to myself and my family that this calling to Africa was not just a mad idea concocted in the heat of student life. My mother was especially skeptical and expressed her disappointment that I planned to "waste my education" by going to the slums of Africa. She had endured deep childhood pain with the breakup of her family and was determined to keep her children nearby.

I felt it was not yet time for me to head to Africa, as certain things needed to fall into place first. Initially, I considered pursuing a postgraduate degree in the United States as a steppingstone to my ultimate goal. However, when I applied for research positions, I was consistently turned down when they heard of my religious convictions and ultimate desire to be a missionary. One person bluntly stated that they did not want any religious people in their research department. In the end, I spent a year teaching at a school in Liverpool, which proved to be a great transition between student life and Africa.

Once, during my time at Malvern College, I had been humiliated during a school debate. When I stood before the hundred or so students, I panicked, forgot all my ideas, and floundered with some lame statements before sitting down red-faced. After that crushing experience, I told myself I would never get involved in any job that included public speaking, teaching, or learning a foreign language. Yet here I was, called to an evangelistic preaching mission where learning multiple languages was essential. I had to surrender my last point of resistance to the Lord. It's marvelous how God can overrule all our phobias by freeing us from fear as we surrender to him. I have spent my adult life frequently speaking in public, utilizing statistics, and learning something of twenty languages, but only preached in four.

Finally, I applied to join the Dorothea Mission and was accepted as a student at their missionary training school in Pretoria, with a view to long-term ministry in the townships of South Africa and surrounding nations.

During the 1962 Easter holidays, I returned home to spend time with my family. While there, I was invited to the home of one of the church elders for coffee after a Sunday service. As we discussed the future, he made an unexpected comment: "I have heard a lady from Essex is planning to go to Africa with the Dorothea Mission." I was surprised, as the mission leaders had not mentioned it to me.

As I absorbed this information, an extraordinary thought came to my mind: "She is going to be your wife!" I believe this was a direct intervention from God himself. I can recall such occurrences only three times in my entire life, so I was shocked. I didn't know her name, what she looked like, or how old she was, so I put this revelation on a mental back burner. This proved to be a wise decision, as I discovered when I reached Africa that the Dorothea Mission had a rule prohibiting single missionaries from marrying until they had served on the field for at least six years!

In September 1962, I began my missionary career by becoming one of the first missionaries to fly to the field in southern Africa. The propeller aircraft I boarded had no cabin pressurization, so we flew at an altitude of just 11,000 feet, which allowed me to look down and see much of the continent of my calling. After three days of flying, including five refueling stops and an overnight stay in Uganda, we arrived in Johannesburg. Little did I know then that this wild and exciting flight would be a glimpse into the life journey that lay ahead of me.

4

HITTING THE GROUND RUNNING— APARTHEID, WITCHCRAFT, AND REVIVAL

Hans von Staden, the Director of the Dorothea Mission, came to Jan Smuts Airport near Johannesburg to pick me up and drive me to Pretoria. How profoundly this man would impact my life! I admired his vision, faith, prayerfulness, and godliness. My life would have been vastly different without his influence; there certainly would not have been an *Operation World*! The first place he took me to was to the African shanty town of Edenvale with its 20,000 people in a square mile with squalor, crime, and smells. It was a an eye-opening and brutal introduction to what would constitute my main ministry for the next sixteen years, but this was where God had called me. It was my first big culture shock!

In 1942, God called Hans and his wife, Lettie, to leave their ministry focused on the white population and to go to the black Africans who were flocking to the cities for work during the rapid industrialization of the Second World War. Tens of thousands of people often crammed into makeshift cardboard and corrugated iron shacks with no amenities, creating places of squalor, deprivation, and crime. Immorality, drug addiction, alcoholism, domestic abuse, and witchcraft were rampant, and it was to these "townships" that I was called to preach Jesus Christ.

The Dorothea Mission's training school produced a stream of local evangelists to reach the black population, and later a second school for missionaries was opened about twenty miles away, where I was based.

In apartheid South Africa, it was illegal for whites and blacks to study together. However, on Saturdays, all sixty of our workers gathered for prayer and Bible study before we went to minister in nearby townships, witnessing door-to-door, holding open-air evangelistic meetings, and distributing gospel tracts. One of our vehicles was an ancient 12-seater minibus, named Hundredfold. The "hundredfold" label aptly described its multiple mechanical deficiencies!

I arrived in Africa at the height of the apartheid era. Most of the white workers in the mission were Afrikaners, and since many lectures at the Bible School were in Afrikaans, I had to quickly become proficient in the language. We foreigners absorbed much of the Afrikaans culture and came to empathize with their heroic yet tragic history, which helped me understand the background behind some of their racial attitudes.

Although I met many great saints and godly Christians among the large number of white evangelical churches, I was baffled by how blind many were to their own views of other races. Perhaps this was not much different from life in the United States at the time, and we had much to learn in Europe about discrimination during the 1960s. A dear South African friend and colleague said of apartheid's terrible psychological wounds: "All of us South Africans of every race need something like a second conversion experience to be free from the effects of apartheid!"

Years later, during a conversation with Hans, he asked me, "How long have we got in South Africa?" I knew exactly what he was asking. I responded based on my research for the early editions of *Operation World*, saying, "Apartheid cannot survive beyond AD 2000." The first fully democratic vote for all races was held in 1994, so my prediction was not far off!

Most people in South Africa believed that violent societal change was inevitable. Yet, when the changes came between 1989 and 1994, there was relatively little violence. I believe this was due to the many Christians praying and actively working for reconciliation. Leaders like Michael Cassidy and Archbishop Desmond Tutu worked tirelessly for reconciliation, hoping to end the decades of pain and violence caused by apartheid.

My first months in Africa were intense. I had to learn to navigate a new set of cultures and understand life in a country dominated by racial separation. Additionally, I encountered some challenges that most missionaries face, contrary to the assumption held by many Christians back home that life in a missions community must be one of bliss and unity.

There was so much to admire about Hans and the Dorothea Mission—the emphasis on faith, prayer, soul-winning, and godly living. I greatly appreciated the fellowship with coworkers who became close friends. However, I also struggled with some negatives: the paternalism and top-down leadership, a distant Mission Council we never met who made decisions for us, and a troubling emphasis on unquestioning loyalty to the leaders, which was considered the highest attribute a worker could possess. The strict adherence to both the legal constraints of the apartheid system and the cultural taboos that accompanied it was a constant source of stress.

In March 1963, it was decided that the missionary students would travel north to the Copperbelt in Zambia, an area with five main towns inhabited by many miners and their families. Extensive deposits of copper had been discovered both in central Zambia and in neighboring areas of the Democratic Republic of Congo. Five mines were developed, making Zambia the largest producer of copper in the world. The wealth of these mines attracted tens of thousands of miners from across Africa and beyond, leading to the establishment of churches to cater to the white businessmen and their families.

We spent an intense month in Kitwe, going door to door inviting people to attend the meetings of a South African evangelist at a large football stadium. The main challenge we encountered was that the Jehovah's Witnesses were already well established in the area, and every home had been visited by them multiple times. I understood why the Apostle Paul said, "It has always been my ambition to preach the gospel where Christ was not known, so that I would not be building on someone else's foundation" (Rom 15:20).

One unexpected feature of my years in Africa was that we erected large tents for meetings that could seat up to four hundred people. We became proficient in erecting, dismantling, transporting, and repairing those tents, many of which we lost due to acts of violence, arson, and storms. Replacing them was very costly. Once, in Rhodesia, we didn't have enough funds for a replacement, so we borrowed a heavy-duty sewing machine, bought canvas and rope, and made our own repairs. I was able to say that I was one of the few truly Pauline missionaries of the twentieth century—a real tent-making missionary!

Our meetings had a strong emphasis on discipling those we led to Christ. We often began with a sizeable crowd of curious people, adults sitting on benches and children on the ground at the front. We would start by singing choruses, all accompanied by an accordion.

The response varied enormously. Sometimes we would pray, witness, and preach with very little result, while at other times we would see many seeking the Lord. As a general observation, Africans are more ready than Westerners to commit themselves to Christ because the spirit world is far more real and present to them.

The biggest struggle people faced was letting go of and ceasing all involvement in ancestor worship and witchcraft. Often, they found deliverance only after publicly renouncing witchcraft. We sometimes held bonfires to burn witchcraft paraphernalia. It was such a deep problem that one pastor confessed he didn't believe the Lord would ever bless his denomination because the pastors practiced witchcraft on each other to gain top leadership positions. My African colleagues told me how preachers sometimes spoke so vigorously that the charms they had purchased to give them power fell out of their pockets!

Once, a missionary from another ministry attended one of our meetings and exclaimed with surprise, "Your African workers are really free from the fear of witchcraft!" I asked him how he could tell, and he responded that they were preaching against it! I often heard our coworkers boldly telling witchdoctors, "I am staying in the house over there. You can try to bewitch me, but it won't work because Jesus lives within me!"

Andrew Murray was a great pioneering missionary in Africa in the late nineteenth century and the author of many wonderful books on prayer. He strongly advocated for churches to hold "Weeks of Prayer for the World" (WoPs) to encourage believers to focus on missions to the unreached rather than their own needs. The leaders of the Dorothea Mission embraced this challenge several years before my arrival in Africa, and WoPs, as they were affectionately known, became regular features of our ministry. Over the next twenty years, many were organized throughout Africa and beyond, contributing to what eventually evolved into *Operation World*.

One afternoon, Hans von Staden summoned me to his home and presented me with a surprising proposition. He asked me to go to Transkei in the Western Cape to organize a Week of Prayer (WoP) in its capital city, Umtata. Transkei was one of two regions in South Africa assigned to the Xhosa people, who are part of the large Bantu group comprising more than eight hundred different tribes and over five hundred distinct languages!

The southern Bantu languages adopted three of the five "click" consonants used by the original Khoisan peoples, which many people first heard while watching the 1980 film *The Gods Must Be Crazy*. Learning these complex languages was challenging, leading to many funny stories. One such story involved a white farmer who believed he was proficient in Zulu and ordered a servant to bring him chicken eggs. Unfortunately, the word for eggs is *amaqanda* (with the click sound represented by a Q), but because he could not pronounce the click, he actually said, *amakhanda* (where the

K sound changed the meaning to "heads"). The bewildered servant returned with severed chicken heads, but no eggs!

I was astonished that Hans entrusted me such a significant responsibility at just twenty-four years old, having only been in Africa for a few months. I was responsible for arranging the program, speakers, and everything else. I felt both honored and overwhelmed by this trust. I was thrown into the deep end; I would either sink or swim!

For me, the entire effort was life-changing, and the Lord helped me see it through to a successful conclusion. It was a timely boost to my confidence, as I had been feeling like a failure. Looking back, I see God's hand preparing me for the future—a ministry of writing a world-changing book. I was learning to develop vital skills for the future, including organizing prayer conferences and relating to a network of diverse people.

How far the Lord had already taken me! I had once vowed never to participate in any ministry that involving public speaking, teaching, or learning foreign languages. Yet the Lord arranged for me to hit the ground running in Africa and dismantled each of my self-imposed barriers. Now I was doing all three!

I had come to serve in South Africa, but within a short time, I unexpectedly found myself involved in ministry in today's Namibia, Zimbabwe, Kenya, Botswana, Lesotho, Zambia, and Mozambique. I later realized that South Africa was a steppingstone placed by God for me to move forward to other needy parts of the unreached world.

My next assignment was to organize a Week of Prayer in Nairobi, Kenya. During my months in Kenya, I heard stories about the East African Revival, straight from the mouths of dear African brothers and sisters associated with this remarkable movement of the Spirit of God. In my estimation, the East African Revival was the purest and longest lasting of all the world's revivals in the twentieth century. It began in 1933 in Rwanda at an Anglican mission station and spread through the surrounding countries in the 1940s and 1950s—particularly Uganda and Kenya, but also into Tanzania, Congo, and South Sudan.

This powerful move of God emphasized being born again through the blood of Jesus, repentance, and restitution. It focused intently on the person of the Lord Jesus, and in response to the people's desire to be more like Christ, the Holy Spirit dealt with issues such as witchcraft, polygamy, lying, racism, and tribal division. God transformed millions of people and brought peace where there had previously been hatred and turmoil. As the revival brethren in Kenya often said, "tribalism and racism were crucified with Jesus on the cross."

While I was organizing a WoP in Kenya, with several prayer meetings scheduled each day, I grew concerned that we had limited background material to stimulate informed prayer. To address this, I put together about six sheets of paper with brief backgrounds on various countries and related prayer needs. When we shared this limited information in the meetings as a prelude to prayer, many people were delighted, having never seen anything like it before. For the first time, I realized what a powerful tool good, printed material could be in the hands of intercessors. It was another steppingstone on the journey toward *Operation World*.

My time in Kenya extended to five months, during which we conducted a three-month tent evangelism campaign in the red-light district of Pumani, Nairobi. We worked closely with the Revival brethren and saw many people come to Jesus. This experience also allowed me to personally witness the handover and celebrations as Kenya transitioned from a British colony to an independent country. Those deeply formative months in Kenya helped me develop unexpected gifts, got me involved in writing about countries, and exposed me to a post-colonial world where mature, godly Africans led the church. I later returned to South Africa with raised expectations of what God would accomplish there and throughout the continent.

5

JILL

As I mentioned previously, before I left Britain for the mission field, a church elder told me that he had heard a lady from Essex was also joining the Dorothea Mission. Although I knew nothing about her at the time, I gradually developed a sense that the Spirit of God had placed the thought in my mind and heart that she would eventually be my wife.

How can I begin to tell the story of this beautiful person whom God loaned to me for twenty-four years? She had a profound influence on my life, my ministry, and, above all, my walk with God.

Jill Amsden and her identical twin sister, June, were born in Essex in 1937. They were very close and did most things together, including their favorite pastime of exploring the nearby Epping Forest. They looked so much alike that few could tell them apart, although June was more controlled and disciplined, earning her the title of the "good" twin. Jill, a mischief-maker, quickly learned how to exploit their resemblance to her maximum benefit, often causing June to be blamed for her sister's escapades.

Their mother, Florence, was a wise woman who skillfully navigated the complexities of raising identical twin daughters. She made sure they were not always in the same class or involved in the same activities, allowing each to develop her own circle of friends. The lifelong, close relationship between the sisters endured, although it was tested by Jill's departure for Africa and the loneliness and hardships she endured in those early years. However, after coming through that difficult period, Jill found a new sense of freedom in a deeper relationship and walk with the Lord Jesus.

When the twins were just three years old, Florence came home one day with a gift for each girl. For June, it was a book titled *A for Angel*, and for Jill, it was *Our Father*. The cover of Jill's book featured a picture of three children walking along a path leading to a charming English village church, with the middle child being a small African boy. At that time, there were few people of African descent in Britain, which piqued Jill's curiosity. She asked her mother about the little boy and learned that he may not have heard about Jesus yet. God planted a seed in Jill's heart, and the vision of bringing Christ to African children ultimately led her to Africa.

When they were 14, the twins were invited to a rally where an evangelist, Tom Rees, shared the gospel. Both were deeply moved and gave their lives to the Lord that evening. Each was then surprised to discover her twin had independently made the same commitment. They became a great source of strength for each other as they grew in their faith.

After completing high school, both Jill and June wanted to become nurses. Nursing was challenging, with 12-hour shifts and only one day off each week. To help remember her lectures, Jill transformed her nursing notes into poetry, making it easier to remember the material. She started her nursing training a year after June did at the same hospital in London. Jill had a soft heart for those around her, and she also had a great sense of fun. One amusing incident occurred when she took advantage of being an identical twin. June and Jill rarely worked together on the same ward. On one occasion, while Jill was still a student nurse and June was already qualified, June was on day shift and Jill on night duty. Neither told their patients that they were twins, so the patients became increasingly concerned that Miss Amsden was working nonstop for 24 hours. The patients were also baffled because it appeared she was being demoted to the rank of student nurse each day, evidenced by her different uniforms!

In June 1962, a friend told Jill about the Dorothea Mission. She contacted the leaders, who accepted her into the ministry. Whereas I had been one of the first missionaries to fly to South Africa, Jill sailed to Cape Town in early 1963, making her one of the last missionaries to go by boat.

Once, I needed to visit the Ladies House in Pretoria, where the female Dorothea missionaries lived. It so happened that Jill was staying there, and when she walked into the room that day, it was the first time I had ever set eyes on her. The memory of what I believed God had told me the previous year in England flooded my mind. This, I realized, was the woman who would one day be my wife!

I wished I could share my thoughts with her, but looming over us was the strict mission rule that prohibited all new recruits from courtship and marriage for at least six years! Even though I disagreed with this rule, I was determined to be loyal to the mission, as I knew God had called me to serve with them. I constantly prayed for grace to help me focus on serving God with an undivided heart.

For the next four years, I said nothing about my feelings to anyone—least of all to Jill herself. My silence meant that I could treat her and the other female missionaries equally as friends and colleagues without embarrassment. However, several eager matchmakers among our colleagues noticed our suitability as a couple and sometimes made things awkward for us.

Despite our isolation, God arranged circumstances that confirmed Jill was the perfect companion for me. One evening, as I struggled with my own inhibitions and began to doubt my call to Africa, Jill walked through the kitchen at the Bible School while I was making a cup of coffee. Although we had barely spoken before, she immediately noticed my distress. Stopping at the door, she turned and quoted Hebrews 4:9: "There remains, then, a Sabbath-rest for the people of God." I responded, "It doesn't work," but she smiled slightly and said, "Yes, it does. Try it!" This was our first personal exchange—a brief but meaningful spiritual interaction.

6

Learning to Walk in the Spirit

Adjusting to life on the mission field came with many ups and downs, especially as God peeled back the layers of my life to expose and heal past baggage and transform wrong motives. At times in my early years, I often struggled to find the way forward.

One major issue I faced was my sense of failure and lack of rest. My teenage years had been deeply miserable, leaving me with feelings of inadequacy and fear that my life would never amount to anything significant. When Jesus entered my life at university, he gave me a sense of purpose and helped me have victory in some areas. Now, I was in Africa doing things I had never dreamed of just a few years earlier, yet my flesh continued to resist as layer after layer of my life was peeled back by the Great Physician.

Throughout this process, I often felt humiliation and shame. I had to repent and allow the Spirit of God to transform me, one sinful, fleshly characteristic at a time. For example, Lettie von Staden shared with me the sad developments in the life of a fellow worker and asked me not to tell anyone. I did not keep my word and let someone else know, who then reported it back to Lettie. When confronted, I was so ashamed and despairing that I contemplated giving up my calling to Africa. During this intense transformative process, ministry in the townships became burdensome due to my inner turmoil and lack of peace, which stripped me of my desire to serve the Lord and love people.

I was also struggling with culture shock in a myriad of ways. For example, I found that many Westerners consider Africans to be liars—not because Africans are dishonest, but because Westerners often misunderstand the cultural framework in which Africans live, where relationships are deeply valued. An African will do everything possible to avoid giving a "No" answer. This often results in either a complete fabrication or a tactful response that doesn't communicate the whole truth. While it may be seen as a face-saving "solution" at the moment, it can lead to misunderstandings and frustration. For instance, if I were to ask an African for directions, he might want to please me with a positive answer, even though he may have no idea where I want to go, leading to meaningless directions. In African thinking, it's better to please me now, even if I become angry later!

Another aspect of African culture that disturbed me was the concept of time. I soon learned that African time typically runs about an hour behind the stated time. Africans are people-oriented and not bound by schedules.

I had more clashes with fellow workers over this issue than any other. I value punctuality and see it as a sign of respect for those I interact with. In African cultures, the people in front of you take precedence over any previously agreed-upon plans. Total attention is given to unexpected guests who may suddenly turn up at the door, even if it means all your colleagues may have to wait and be late for a meeting. Africans would tell me, "You Westerners have your clocks, but we have the time!"

One night, while reflecting on the rest of God that Jill had mentioned, I got out of bed and went into the bathroom to spend some time alone with the Lord, not wanting to disturb my roommates. I was drawn to read the words of the risen Jesus to the Laodiceans, and I realized that his rebuke was aimed directly at my own spiritual state at that time. I thought I was a success, but in truth I was lukewarm. As the Holy Spirit shone a spotlight on my heart, I began to see that much of what I had achieved was done in my own strength, without consciously depending on Jesus. He desired to be the Lord of every part of my life, and I needed to learn to rest and trust in him. I knew I had been saved from sin and judgment by God's grace, but I was largely living as if my own efforts would produce fruit in ministry. I had to learn to *live* by grace, not just be *saved* by grace. What freedom that truth gave me!

During this time, I was greatly blessed and encouraged by the writings of Norman Grubb, who led the Worldwide Evangelization Crusade (now WEC International) for over two decades after the death of C. T. Studd, its famous founder. Grubb's many books exposed me to a deeper level of walking in the Spirit. This revelation led to a breakthrough in my faith, and I realized that instead of focusing on any specific spiritual gift, I should ask God for the Holy Spirit, as it is up to him to dispense gifts as it pleases him. As I simply asked God to fill me, I experienced a deep peace and expectation that he would use me in a special way and give me the power to do what he called me to do. I returned to the work in the townships with a heightened expectation of fruitfulness. I believe this was borne out in the following years.

During the years I was involved with tent ministry, we intentionally did not try to plant churches. Instead, our strategy was to stay in an area long enough to lead people to Christ, begin discipling them, and then connect them with a local church that we hoped would nurture them in their faith. This meant we sought to establish good relationships with local churches both before and during our visits, but the results were mixed, as few churches were equipped to properly nurture and disciple new believers.

Over the years, this lack of success in establishing new converts in their faith made me more passionate about discipleship—more than simply winning souls! After all, discipling the nations is the key ministry Jesus gave us in the Great Commission. I would rather have twelve disciples who stay the course and impact the world than have 100,000 lukewarm converts!

In March 1965, I contracted hepatitis B, and for five weeks, I was so ill that I fainted every time I attempted to stand. I turned a shade of yellow and lay prostrate for weeks. Typically, the disease requires six weeks of bed rest followed by at least another six weeks of recuperation. However, Hans von Staden visited me in the fifth week and asked if I could lead a team to conduct an outreach in Durban, even if it meant I did so from my bed. Wanting to appear brave and committed, I foolishly agreed to lead the team. I should have declined, but I struggled to say "no," especially to those I felt I owed a debt of loyalty.

The month that followed brought a series of disasters. The team I led to Durban was ill-prepared. We arrived tired, disunified, and without much prayer. We pitched our tent on a small hill among the houses and preached for a month but didn't see anyone come to Christ. Two of our female workers even had a loud verbal fight in the street in front of the very people we wanted to reach.

During that trip, I was both too ill and too inexperienced to cope effectively. However, from that time on, I became passionate about pre-campaign prayer and made sure that teams were united before the Lord. The Holy Spirit fell on the disciples in the book of Acts when they were together, united in prayer. We did not always achieve this, but it became my goal!

I learned some harsh lessons from the fallout of contracting hepatitis. The Bible says, "Desire without knowledge is not good, how much more will hasty feet miss the way" (Prov 19:2). I learned that prescribed rest periods after a serious illness are there for a reason, and l believe my unwise decision delayed my full recovery for years. My pulse rate did not return to normal levels for about seven years.

(7)

1964—THE FIRST *OPERATION WORLD*

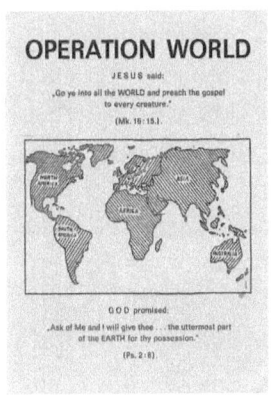

After returning to South Africa from my five-month stint in Kenya, I shared with Hans von Staden everything that had happened there, including the new info-sheets I had created to help people intercede during our Week of Prayer gatherings. The same information was used at a special "Three Weeks of Prayer" conference in July 1964, held at the Victoria Falls in Rhodesia. The third week was specifically set aside for African Christians, with services conducted in their native languages. It was a moving experience to see over one hundred Africans on their knees interceding for parts of the world many had never heard of before!

Hans was enthusiastic and encouraged me to compile the information into a booklet. He even suggested a title for it: "*Operation World*." I spent the next several months researching, refining, and rewriting the information I had used in Kenya. During this process, I received help from nine inter-denominational ministries in South Africa. This principle of inclusiveness set a pattern that continued for the next half century.

By inviting Christian leaders from various doctrinal persuasions to contribute, they felt involved in the process. When the books finally appeared, much of the body of Christ viewed them as a resource they had helped create. Consequently, a wide range of denominations and missions felt comfortable endorsing *Operation World* as a valuable resource for their members.

I feel privileged to have been influenced by the three-stranded spiritual heritage of Reformed Christianity, with its emphasis on God's sovereignty and the exposition of his Word; the Holiness stream, with its strong emphasis on the need for sanctification and holy living; and the Pentecostal-Charismatic stream, with its emphasis on the present working of the Holy Spirit through his gifts and an expectation that God will reveal his presence and power to us each day. These three streams combined to provide a robust theological framework for my writing about the church and its ministry, and I sense that I "belong" to all three. Perhaps this is why all the major streams of evangelical Christianity felt comfortable using *Operation World*.

The basic template for future editions of *Operation World* was established during this time. Each country was given a brief introduction with essential information and core statistics, followed by relevant prayer items. One reason for this format was my inability to obtain comprehensive information to fully address all aspects of the spiritual needs of countries. However, this structure allowed me to include a summary of what I had at the time and provide further information and prayer needs in the subsequent prayer points. This proved to be a good model for decades, with the information and data in each subsequent edition becoming more effective and authoritative. Over time, *Operation World* became the go-to resource for Christians around the world seeking a Christian perspective on specific countries.

With my love of maps, I wanted to make sure each continent was accompanied by an informative map. In what may sound extraordinary to most people today, during the pre-computer era, I drew all the maps by hand on tracing paper. The results were amateurish but adequate! My classmates and I typed the information onto wax sheets for duplication on a Gestetner duplicating machine—photocopiers had also not yet been invented! The sheets were then cut and collated into an A5-sized booklet for use in subsequent Weeks of Prayer for the World gatherings.

Hans von Staden wrote an enthusiastic foreword for the first-ever *Operation World*, which included:

> We have been mightily impressed by the powerful intercessions of the Weeks of Prayer gatherings for Africa ... A peak, no doubt, was reached in the third of the three weeks of prayer at the Victoria Falls in Rhodesia in July 1964. To see 100 Africans on their knees for eight days crying to God for all the continents—within the sound of the mighty roar of the Falls—was an unforgettable memory.

We had to ask ourselves: "Does God want such prayers to be limited to Africa?" This is a critical time in world history. All nations are in peril. Never was the Gospel more needed ... Where are the mighty conversions? Where is a great spiritual advance? How God's people everywhere must pray for this doomed world! Only prayer can prevent fast approaching chaos.

It is interesting to read Hans's words written over half a century ago. His warnings about approaching chaos were not hyperbole. The remaining years of the 1960s brought chaos and bloodshed to post-colonial Africa, Mao's Cultural Revolution in China, and the spread of Communism across many parts of the world.

I believe the tumult in the world provided fertile ground for the subsequent massive turning to God in Africa, China, parts of Central Asia, Iran, Algeria, and Indonesia. The prayers of the saints are enormously impactful, rising like incense to God's altar, bringing down the fires of both judgment and revival, like when the seventh seal was opened in the eighth chapter of Revelation.

In 1792, just before he sailed to India, the great missionary pioneer William Carey wrote the first survey of the world, making a passionate plea for Protestant churches to become involved in spreading the gospel to the nations. The last part of Carey's book, *An Enquiry into the Obligations of Christians to Use Means for the Conversion of the Heathens*, contained a global survey of every known country and region. This marked the beginning of the modern missionary movement as we know it today, founded on thorough Christian research.

More than 170 years after Carey's groundbreaking book, I was astonished to find that there was not a subsequent single publication that covered the statistics and religions of the nations of the world from a Christian perspective. I could not find a book on the state of Christianity in each country or a listing of all the people groups of the world. I saw a significant need in the body of Christ, and I hoped the Lord would use me to help fill that gap.

By the mid-1960s, God had raised up several key researchers, including Donald McGavran, a missionary to India and prolific author; David Barrett, an English Anglican priest based in Kenya who was beginning his remarkable research into the global church; and Leslie Lyall, a long-time missionary to China who was busy researching his book, *A World to Win*, published in 1967. I have borrowed from his choice of title for this book!

Finally, to round out the emerging wave of mission resources that would help shape global Christianity in the next generation, the Wycliffe Bible Translators published their second *Ethnologue* book in 1965. This misnamed book is not a listing of ethnic groups as the title suggests, but rather of languages. It more accurately should have been called a "Lingualogue"! Nevertheless, this resource became an indispensable tool for Christian researchers, Bible translators, and church planters. Over the years, I have been an avid user and contributor to the *Ethnologue* and its authoritative listing of every known language in the world. It has gone through 23 editions, first in book form and now entirely as an online subscription service. In 1969, the *Ethnologue* listed 4,493 languages, and by 2024, that number had grown to 7,164 languages in use worldwide.

With all these research streams—and others—converging simultaneously, the time was right for the first *Operation World*. It was typeset and printed in Germany and then used extensively for the next few years in many prayer gatherings in Africa and Europe. It was a relief to finally see the book in print, and I prayed that the Lord Jesus would breathe on *Operation World* and cause it to be a useful tool to aid the completion of the Great Commission.

As the book went global, I had to learn to be both bold and diplomatic, ensuring that readers did not feel slighted or unduly offended in my attempts to portray every country effectively. For example, the divided territory of Kashmir was listed under both contesting countries, India and Pakistan, and Taiwan was separated from China because the government in Taipei controls the island. I sought to be scrupulously objective, especially in controversial areas, to encourage acceptance of the book regardless of a reader's political opinions or national background.

Over the years, I have observed that when most people pick up a copy of *Operation World* for the first time, they invariably turn to the country they know best. If the information on that page is not credible, they may reject the entire book. Therefore, I had to ensure that the data for each country was accurate and verifiable, while the text and prayer points informed and inspired readers to pray.

8

Rhodesia

One way you can know you have been around for a while is when the names of countries and places where you have lived no longer exist due to political changes and revolutions. For most of the twelve years from 1966 to 1978, I was based in Rhodesia, now called Zimbabwe, spending my first three years in the capital city, Salisbury, which is now known as Harare. My initial three years in South Africa were filled with both blessing and trauma. I felt like a schoolteacher who started my career making so many mistakes that it compromised my credibility with that generation of students. A move to another school could offer a fresh start!

I pondered how I could make that fresh start and prayed about the possibility of working in one of the Dorothea Mission fields outside South Africa. Increasingly, I thought about Rhodesia, which was ruled by a white minority government that had recently shocked the world by unilaterally declaring independence from Britain. There was also racial discrimination in Rhodesia, but it was more subtle than in South Africa. In some ways, I feel that South Africa in the 1960s paralleled the *legal* racial discrimination of the southern United States at that time, while Rhodesian society resembled the *social* discrimination seen in the rest of America.

For instance when we, as Dorothea workers in Rhodesia traveled to South Africa once or twice a year to attend our mission gatherings, and we always dreaded crossing the Limpopo River into South Africa. We faced numerous petty humiliations, uncertainty about how the police would treat us, and a never-ending sense of being watched! I was always on the alert to protect my fellow workers from these irritations during our travels.

I was approached by Hans and Lettie von Staden and asked if I would be willing to lead tent campaigns in the towns and cities of Rhodesia. Our first Bible school students were completing their training and were eager to start ministering. I was rather excited and a bit daunted by the request, as I would be responsible for building an effective multicultural team of raw recruits.

In early October 1966, I headed north in our big van to the Dorothea Mission Bible School, which had about a dozen African students at the time, some of whom came from broken families and violent backgrounds. The school became my base for the next six years—a period I consider a blessed time in my life. I enjoyed the relative freedom of living and ministering there compared to the claustrophobic atmosphere of apartheid South Africa.

At that time of its founding, Rhodesia had a population of around 500,000 people in an area twice the size of the United Kingdom. The territory was named after colonialist Cecil Rhodes and was divided into Northern Rhodesia (now Zambia) and Southern Rhodesia (Zimbabwe). After multitudes of British settlers occupied and developed the best agricultural land and abundant minerals, Rhodesia quickly became a prosperous British colony, with wealth concentrated in the hands of the white settlers.

A year before I moved there, Rhodesia unilaterally declared independence from Britain. In response, the United Nations imposed sanctions on the country, leading to massive social disruption. This chaotic political landscape greeted me when I arrived in 1966. During my years in Rhodesia, a growing African independence movement led to civil war and ultimately to independence under majority rule in 1980. These political and economic upheavals affected both our ministry and my writing of two editions of *Operation World*.

Looking back at the precious team God assembled in Rhodesia, I feel privileged to have known each member. They included Moffatt Ncube, who had been a teenage gangster, and

Steve Lungu, who, as a young man, had harbored an overwhelming ambition to find and kill the mother who had deserted him as a boy. Steve tried to burn down the Dorothea Mission's tent with a firebomb in 1962, but the Lord took hold of his life before he could do it. In many ways, Steve became my "Timothy" in Africa. He later became a great Christian leader, renowned across the world as a powerful speaker. His gripping testimony is told in his biography, *Out of the Black Shadows*.

Our team also included a blind brother named Josias Ngara, who lost his sight to measles at the age of five. His mother was strict with him and forced him to fend for himself. He learned to cook, chop firewood, wash clothes, and clean his room. He walked everywhere without a stick, using his remaining senses to compensate for his lack of sight. Whenever we changed locations, he quickly learned the local geography and could even guide us through the streets when it was pitch dark.

Our team had a mixture of stormy and good times as we tried to break down cultural and racial barriers. It took years to dismantle the "us" and "them" mentality, with our African coworkers often condoning and concealing sin from me as their leader because they didn't want to "betray" one another to a white man. We had to learn to trust one another, which led to some rocky times, but I came to value and appreciate each member as a dear friend and colleague.

After our third month of campaigning, we had seen little fruit, and few people showed any evidence of new life in Jesus. My team blamed me because I was the one who had decided where to preach. Recognizing that our team dynamics needed an urgent overhaul if we were to be successful, I suggested something considered radical at the time. I encouraged greater participation from all team members, and decisions were to be made only after the entire group took everything to God in prayer. This shift marked a significant departure from the typical mission practices of that era and completely transformed the atmosphere within the team.

Later, we extended this principle of openness to our financial matters, ensuring everyone was fully aware of our team finances—both ministry operating expenses and our personal allowances. We were often desperately short of funds, but financial transparency prevented disputes among us. Everything was brought into the light, where misconceptions could not thrive. Team members knew that, although I had a larger allowance—about double theirs—I lived frugally and reinvested much into the work, so everyone benefitted.

The changes we implemented in Rhodesia prompted me to question the broader culture of our Dorothea Mission. In the 1960s, there was an unspoken paternalistic belief that our African members needed white leadership to become effective. Discussions about Africans taking on leadership roles or eventually taking charge were minimal. After much thought and prayer regarding our team's long-term goals, I wrote a ten-point plan for implementing a complete handover to our African brothers within ten years. I shared the plan in a letter to Hans von Staden, but he never replied. I took his silence as approval!

In today's globalized world, multicultural teams are common, often employing an equal partnership model between nationals and expatriates. Numerous books, seminars, and experts now exist to help organizations facilitate such teams effectively. Back then, we had to prayerfully navigate uncharted territory, learning from our mistakes along the way. The Lord helped us grow and succeed, and we saw God perform many miracles as he provided for our needs in unexpected ways. These principles became integral to the life and ministry of my fellow workers in their subsequent ministry careers.

Our team really was like a big family in many ways. I invested considerable time teaching Steve and Moffatt how to organize a campaign, negotiate with officials, keep basic accounts, drive, and perform a myriad of other tasks. I even bought a piano accordion and taught myself how to play it to lead worship in our meetings, but they soon replaced me with their better musical gifts.

While there was much to celebrate in our work, we encountered many crises along the way. One particularly dire situation occurred when one of our female South African workers was courted by a Malawian without my knowledge. I unwittingly acted as the mailman for the letters that passed between them since the young man used my address. When he wrote asking if he could join our team for a month, I asked my coworkers if there were any reasons he shouldn't come. They assured me there was no problem, concealing the real reason for his coming. His visit resulted in the young lady becoming pregnant. Several of the team members had deliberately deceived me and were subsequently disciplined and removed from the work for months. This incident nearly caused a complete breakdown of trust within the team. However, after much pain, repentance, and healing, we emerged as a smaller team with far less racial division.

For the next twelve years, we crisscrossed the country, holding tent campaigns in towns and cities across Rhodesia. We generally spent about a month in one location, holding meetings every evening. This approach enabled us to evangelize the lost and begin discipling new believers.

I made a real effort to become proficient in four local languages, although my fellow workers preferred that I preach in English with interpretation during the meetings, because it carried more weight with the better educated in the audience. Nevertheless, the value of learning the heart languages of the people we sought to reach was invaluable. As the independence war escalated, my presence within the team became a point of controversy for locals; but once people found out I spoke their language, the political issues waned in importance!

As we visited nearly every town in Rhodesia over the years, I acquired a wealth of information, and produced a survey of the languages of Zimbabwe, the progress of the gospel, and the future challenges that lay ahead. This had never been done before, so I distributed printed copies of my survey at a conference of Christian leaders.

The greatest challenge people faced was reaching the point where they were so convinced of the power and reality of Jesus Christ that they were willing to leave the generations of ancestor worship and witchcraft behind. Until they experienced that breakthrough, many people were prone to falling away from the faith. The key to lasting conversions took place when believers truly embraced the fact that the Lord Jesus Christ was now living in their hearts and was truly stronger than all the forces of darkness.

We witnessed many exciting and amazing conversions in Rhodesia. Many who were transformed from darkness to light became pastors or missionaries, and years later, I became aware of some of the lasting fruit that was produced. Three testimonies stand out.

First, in 1968, a remarkable conversion of a male schoolteacher took place in a town called Chiredzi. The teacher's wife attended almost every night of our meetings, but he would turn up at the end of the service, drunk and angry, intent on causing a disturbance. We prayed for God's intervention, and as our month in Chiredzi came to a close, the teacher approached me and asked, "How can God forgive me when I have taught seventy-three children that there is no God?" In our subsequent conversation about God's forgiveness, he came to faith and testified that he surrendered his life to Jesus Christ on our last evening there.

Second, Saluh Daka was a young transvestite who came to one of our tent meetings in Bulawayo. He repented and gave his life to Jesus, and in 1976, he joined a YWAM team to Mozambique during a chaotic period as the Portuguese handed over the country to the Communist guerillas. Saluh was arrested for handing out Bibles on the street and imprisoned. Somehow, he managed to escape and walked to the coast, where he borrowed a small boat. He rowed out to sea, hoping to escape to South Africa, but when he got through the breakers, he realized he didn't know which way to go, so he returned and surrendered. Eventually, he was released, married a Dutch woman, and they served as missionaries in Gabon, Central Africa. While there, he contracted malaria and died. Years later, I was moved to see a plaque in his honor at the YWAM base in Amsterdam.

The third testimony is about Oliver Nyumbu, who was a schoolboy when he placed his trust in God and started his journey with the Lord, but I didn't hear anything about him for many years. Then, in 1980, I received an invitation to speak at the YWAM base in Haywards Heath, in southern England. I was astonished when the Zimbabwean leader stood up before I spoke and said, "I want to introduce you to my father in the Lord! He may not remember me, but he led me to Jesus in Zimbabwe, and I am now serving God in England as a result!" This deeply moved me. Here I was, seeking to recruit British people for missions work, and one I had led to Jesus in Africa was now a missionary in my homeland!

The process of handing over leadership to local believers in Rhodesia was not simple. At times, we had significant tension on our team, and I became aware of strong feelings against me and the other white members. Steve Lungu was deeply resentful, believing that I always picked on and criticized him, which caused him to walk around looking miserable and angry much of the time. I think I was firmer with Steve because he was so talented and obviously a future leader.

Looking back, I realize how little I understood about team dynamics and cultural challenges. I had not taken the time to understand the impact of Steve's devastating childhood, and his deep need for acceptance and value after being rejected by both parents and living for years as a street kid. In later years, much of my life involved starting, leading, training, and coming alongside multicultural teams, so I am grateful for the hard lessons I learned in Rhodesia.

9

THE LONG PATH TO MARRIAGE

I was acutely aware of the mission rule that prohibited courting between missionaries for six years. Although I saw Jill as my perfect life companion, I wanted to be faithful to the Dorothea Mission in every respect. I constantly prayed for the grace to remain true to that commitment and focused on serving the Lord with an undivided heart. My silence allowed me to build warm relationships with all the students and fellow workers, including Jill, who remained unaware of my interest in her. This helped prevent her heart from going in a direction that could cause her grief and result in us breaking the rules of the mission.

There was a deep peace in my heart that God would preserve Jill during those years of waiting, despite other prospective suitors. Little did I know, until years later, the agonies she endured. Unknown to me, a young woman heard me testify about my calling at a public meeting soon after my arrival and became infatuated with me, even joining the mission because of this. She soon realized that Jill would be her greatest rival and set out to damage Jill's reputation through distortions and lie, hoping to force her to leave the mission. Unfortunately, these accusations were not handled correctly, and Jill came under suspicion as a "Communist." As a result, this same woman was paired with Jill for a few years as a "chaperone." Jill never said a word to our leaders about what was going on, but those years were hard and lonely for her. This experience had the deep effect of weaning her from dependence on people—something important for an identical twin—and fostered a deep trust in the companionship of Jesus.

Jill worked on teams in several cities and saw many children come to Christ. One time, her team was working in the township of Pinetown near Durban, where they experienced a deep work of God's Spirit, with many children surrendering their lives to the Lord. A young Zulu boy named Beaumont was on his way to commit a robbery with his gang when he was distracted by the tent meeting. He went inside, was convicted of his sins, and gave his heart to the Lord. Beaumont's life was so transformed that he soon began preaching in the streets and became known as the "boy street preacher." Some rival teenage gang members became jealous, and they attacked and murdered him. Beaumont was a martyr for Jesus.

Some time later, I visited the Pretoria home of a godly Baptist pastor, Victor Thomas, and his wife, Burnie. They knew both Jill and me separately and had privately thought we were well-suited for each other. When Burnie stood up and closed the living room door, I instinctively knew she was going to talk to me about Jill. I was determined to remain silent about my feelings for Jill and prayed in my heart for an interruption. At that very moment, Burnie's son came into the room, and the moment passed.

The following year, I visited Burnie again, but in the meantime, a colleague had shared with me the agonies that Jill had endured. This time my reluctance to speak had gone, so when Burnie closed the same door, I knew Jill would be the topic of conversation. I shared my belief that Jill was God's special choice for me. Burnie exclaimed, "I must tell Jill!" to which I forcefully responded, "No, you must not!" I didn't want to compromise the occasional times of friendly contact I had with Jill by embarrassing her, even though those opportunities were rare since I was now based in Rhodesia, more than one thousand miles away. We agreed that she would only tell Jill if Jill specifically asked to visit her. The next day, Jill phoned Burnie to ask if she could stay the night in their home. At the time we had two teams holding tent meetings in different parts of Soweto, Johannesburg. On Monday, we had a combined prayer meeting for both teams, so we arrived at one of the tents in two separate vehicles. I saw Jill sitting in the passenger seat of a van, and she waved at me. Immediately, by the way she waved, I knew that Burnie had told Jill of my feelings for her. The cat was out of the bag!

A few months later, I returned to South Africa. Jill and I had mutual friends who had moved to Durban. I phoned them and asked if I could stay in their home for several nights, as I needed to buy a vanload of gospel literature to take back to Rhodesia. When I arrived, I was greeted with knowing grins and told, "We know why you wanted to stay. Jill is coming to visit us tomorrow!"

I hadn't realized Jill was in Durban, but instead of feeling exhilarated, the news that I would see her deeply troubled me. I couldn't trust myself to remain silent, and I still had nearly two years of my six-year relationship exile left before I could make any move toward marriage! Moreover, it concerned me that my hosts thought I had planned this operation to circumvent the rules and meet with Jill.

That night, I prayed earnestly that Jill might delay her visit. As I prayed, I heard the phone ring in the hallway. Apparently, Jill had been taken sailing on the Indian Ocean, got badly sunburned, and couldn't come. When asked if I would like to speak with Jill on the phone, I found myself in a dilemma. God had answered my prayer, but I needed to remain loyal to the mission rules, so I said, "No, thank you." Later, Jill told me how deeply upset and confused she was. Here was the man whom she had heard was professing love for her, yet he wouldn't even speak with her on the phone. When I returned to Pretoria, I explained the situation to Burnie. She then informed Jill, which somewhat reassured her.

The six-year isolation period still had much time to run, and the mission had also decreed that all new missionaries must complete an initial six-year term on the field before they could return home for home leave. It seemed logical to me that Jill and I should combine our home visit with a wedding.

My plan was for both of us to return to the United Kingdom for our leave, where we could celebrate our marriage with family and friends before returning to Africa as newlyweds. This would be a particularly significant event for Jill's family. All three Amsden daughters were in their thirties, and Jill would be the first to walk down the aisle. However, my well-laid plans soon ran into some major obstacles, and many twists and turns awaited us before we finally reached the altar!

I wrote to the von Stadens to ask for permission to have some contact with Jill with a view to possible marriage. I thought this would give us a few days to connect after the annual mission conference in September, which appeared to be the only opportunity for Jill and me to meet before we left for England in September 1968. I received a cautious and rather stern response from Hans von Staden. He granted me a "concession" to meet with Jill after the conference, but I was not permitted to correspond with her until I returned to Rhodesia, a safe distance of a thousand miles away!

Finally, the day arrived when I would see my beloved Jill face-to-face. We had a memorable first meeting, and I didn't waste much time before asking the obvious question: "Will you marry me?" She responded demurely, saying, "I think we first ought to pray over it." We went for walks and spoke freely during the three wonderful days that followed. These were precious moments, and we covered a lot of ground. For almost six years, we had been distant acquaintances in the same ministry, but we had never shared more than fleeting words.

On our final day together, Jill had hardly slept the night before. When I pressed for the reason, she confided that her family was very affectionate. I took the hint, realizing that I had not yet given her a hug or a kiss. I explained that touching her would be like holding fire in my hands, and I wanted to love her honorably. As we parted that evening for our long separation, however, we leaned toward each other and shared our first brief kiss!

It wasn't until I was driving across the Limpopo Plateau back to Rhodesia with my team that I realized Jill had not given a clear answer. Although we had talked about marriage and her willingness seemed evident, she had never actually said "yes" to my proposal. However, I soon received the affirmation I needed when Jill's first letter since our separation arrived. In it, she penned a poem, which came just a few weeks after Dr. Christian Barnard made worldwide headlines by performing the first human heart transplant at a hospital in South Africa. She wrote:

> *You see I thought it grand*
> *When you asked me for my hand.*
> *But when you did depart*
> *You also stole my heart.*
> *New heart transplantings make good news*
> *But how much worse your heart to lose.*
> *So now my heart is far away*
> *I sit disheartened all the day.*
> *But I am sure that with this letter*
> *The situation will be much better!*

Although our plans to join our lives together had taken their first tentative steps, the following four months turned out to be a series of nightmares for Jill and me. Thankfully, we didn't have to endure this alone, as we shared our struggles in nearly daily letters. These letters served as a lifeline and laid a solid foundation for understanding each other. We shared deeply about who we really were—both the serious stuff and the more humorous. We also wrote a lot about our desires as a couple and the likelihood of becoming parents.

In one letter, I shared my concern about having very flat feet. They are so flat that when I walk with wet feet and lift my toes, it's not easy to tell which foot has left its imprint. I warned Jill that my flat feet might be part of my DNA and might be passed on to our children. She responded with another of her brilliant poems:

> *My dearest Pat, whose feet are flat,*
> *Do not try to heal your arches with medicinal starches.*
> *It was not for your toes that my hand has chose,*
> *Nor is it your feet that make my life complete,*
> *But I have truly found*
> *That you suit me to the ground!*

As soon as I arrived back in Rhodesia, we were plunged into the worst team crisis of my sixteen years in Africa. Nearly all our team members were in their twenties, with raging hormones, resulting in several moral failures that ruined some of their lives. To top it off, one of the Bible school staff also had a serious lapse in morality, leaving the other leaders and me distraught. We had poured our lives into these dear colleagues, aiming to build them up for future leadership roles, but now it seemed like a lost cause. It came as a relief when three of the workers we had placed under discipline chose not to leave the ministry but to go through the public humiliation and sense of failure. In due time, they were restored and became valuable workers in the years that followed.

The exhilaration I felt each time I received a letter from Jill was counterbalanced by a series of grim letters from Hans von Staden. When I sought permission to meet with Jill during the summer holidays, Hans firmly refused. He was shocked by the news of the moral failures on the Rhodesia team and was unwilling to relax the rules, fearing that Jill and I might join the list of those who had stumbled into sin. We had to set an example of transparency and purity for our African workers.

Hans repeated that we had already been granted a concession to write to each other, and no further allowances would be made. All efforts to see Jill were thwarted, much to our frustration. It was difficult to see how we could plan our wedding under such circumstances. In the end, we submitted to the restrictions and prayed that our wedding plans would somehow fall into place.

Then, when all hope of seeing Jill before our departures from Africa appeared to be lost, Lettie von Staden casually mentioned that they had not intended for Jill and me to have no face-to-face contact at all. This was news to me! We quickly arranged for Jill to stay with her friends in Pretoria, allowing us to spend five more precious days together. We made a timeline for planning our wedding ceremony so that our families and close friends could attend.

During our days together, we also bought an opal engagement ring, but we had to leave it with the von Stadens since we were still officially required to keep our relationship secret until they decided it appropriate to make a public announcement. The mission leaders were determined to uphold their six-year rule. Nobody could formally know of our engagement until that period had run its full course!

I realize that the extraordinary romance and rigid rules Jill and I endured may sound strange and perhaps even ridiculous to many people today, but it was the world in which we then lived. At least we can look back and know that we did everything we could to walk in the light and maintain purity before marriage. At times, I think I gained an understanding of how Jacob must have felt about Rachel, for whom he had to wait seven years. The Bible says: "So Jacob served seven years for Rachel, and they seemed only a few days to him because of the love he had for her" (Gen 29:20).

As we walked through the long process, Jill and I learned more about forgiving others and about our own hearts. I believe we became better servants of God, and the trials we experienced in getting to the altar contributed to a truly great marriage!

Oddly, the first time Jill and I realized our engagement was official was when we read it in the Dorothea Mission's circular letters to workers in early June 1968. We wrote congratulatory letters to each other, and Jill rushed to headquarters as soon as she could to retrieve her ring! She was overjoyed to have this evidence of our commitment and took great care of the ring. Several months later, however, Jill and her team were returning home from meetings in Northern Transvaal when they stopped for lunch. Jill took off the ring and carefully placed it on the hood of their little car so she could wash her hands, but then forgot to retrieve it. They finished their meal and drove off. About twenty-five miles later, Jill looked down at her unadorned ring finger in horror!

They quickly drove back to the place they had eaten but could not find the ring. Then Jill had an idea. She found a stone that was about the same size as the ring and placed it on the same spot on the hood. They drove off at a comparable speed while scanning the road ahead. When the stone fell off the car, they slowed down and searched more carefully. Several miles later, as they drove down the main street of the little town of Nelspruit, someone spotted the ring in the middle of the road. No one had seen it, and no vehicle had run over it. The ring was triumphantly returned to Jill's finger with much praise to the Lord for answered prayer!

10

MARRIED LIFE AND MINISTRY

If Jill and I had expected a peaceful and relaxed period leading up to our wedding day, we were sorely disappointed! The children's work in South Africa suddenly blossomed in the months just prior to Jill's departure for England, leaving her to spend every spare moment managing the growth of that ministry.

In Rhodesia, we also experienced many breakthroughs in those months, although my lingering memories are clouded by my contracting malaria in mid-winter—a rare occurrence—that troubled me for many years with recurring low-grade fevers.

The success of the children's ministry inspired Hans von Staden, who suddenly came up with a plan that required Jill to join him on a publicity tour of major European cities: Berlin, Paris, Amsterdam, Brussels, Zurich, and, of course, London. Hans was determined to fit all those meetings in before Christmas 1968, but he also needed us to participate in the annual mission conference in South Africa in late September, which would be attended by over one thousand guests.

The timing could not have been worse for us. Jill and I were utterly exhausted after the unrelenting demands of six years in the ministry. Our families were already planning to attend our wedding on October 19, and this hectic new schedule would leave us with only three weeks to plan our big day after arriving in Britain. We felt pressured to accept the new plan. In retrospect, we should have firmly told Hans, "No!"

As if we were not already stressed enough, Hans then dropped a bombshell by announcing that an unspecified crisis had arisen in the ministry, and he was unable to go on the European trip. He asked me to take over the entire tour, including all the planning. In this era before email, arrangements had to be made by letter, so weeks passed as we contacted people in each European city where we had been asked to go.

Finally, after fulfilling all our commitments in South Africa, Jill and I flew back to the United Kingdom—together! Our respective parents welcomed us at the airport, and despite surviving those days on adrenaline, we appreciated catching up with our loved ones for the first time in six years.

By the sustaining grace of God, we finally made it to the altar and were joined together in Christ at Buckhurst Hill Baptist Church on the scheduled date of October 19, 1968. Glyn Davies, the Dorothea Mission representative who helped mobilize us to go to Africa, shared a message from Philippians 1:21: "For me, to live is Christ and to die is gain."

I managed to buy a Ford Anglia for £100. It was nearing the end of its life, but it became a dependable vehicle for the duration of our stay in the United Kingdom. We drove north for a brief honeymoon in the Lake District—five days of bliss. The time was far too short, but it was precious. The strangest feeling for us was being alone and not surrounded by other people. Life in Africa is always lived in community and is noisy, hectic, and often messy—but never boring. We could have used several months of peace and quiet, but due to our commitment, we flew to Germany to begin a month of constant meetings and travel.

During the year Jill and I had spent corresponding by letter, we shared much about the possibility of starting a family. Jill loved children and jokingly said she had completed the first two parts of midwife training, so now she wanted to move on to the third—giving birth herself!

We had no accommodation arranged for our return to Africa, and I was concerned that we shouldn't start a family too quickly before everything was in place. Jill assured me it was unlikely she would become pregnant quickly and that I shouldn't worry about it. She was an optimist. Before the end of our hastily arranged ministry tour of Europe, Jill discovered she was "late" and began to experience morning sickness. The next stage of our rollercoaster ride with the Lord included a honeymoon baby!

Having been isolated from the rest of the world by the nature of the ministry we were involved in, we found we had returned home to a very different society. There had been many changes in our families, our churches, and the cultures of Europe. We had missed so much of the culture of the era—the Beatles and the songs people sang, the Charismatic wave in the churches, and the changes in worship styles across denominations.

Our seven months on home assignment had not been wasted. Three young men were recruited to join the mission, and more prayer and interest were mobilized to help advance the gospel in southern Africa. However, as our time drew to a close and our return to Africa neared, feelings of excitement and dread came upon us.

The Dorothea Mission possessed many great qualities—a strong emphasis on prayer, godly living, and winning souls for Christ. But we were also aware of its dysfunctions. We found ourselves living in the shadow of the leader-founders, who ran the mission as a kind of paternalistic, benign dictatorship. A Nazarene missionary once spoke with Hans and said, "You should prepare someone to take over the leadership," to which Hans replied, "No, I will remain leader until I die!"

Looking back with the benefit of hindsight, the Dorothea Mission was a tough school for training in godliness. Hans was a complex individual—brilliant and caring, but also deeply fearful of worker failures and of the apartheid-era South African authorities and secret police. Coming from a German immigrant family where discipline and strictness were highly valued, these factors combined to produce the rules-based, autocratic ministry into which Jill and I had invested so much of our lives. It's remarkable how many of our colleagues who moved on to other ministries seemed to flourish and become more fruitful in their new environments!

There were many things we wish could have been done differently, but at the same time, we know that God advanced his kingdom through the mission, and without this remarkable ministry, *Operation World* would never have come into existence.

During our time in England, I visited Bulstrode, a huge stately home that served as the headquarters of WEC International in Gerrards Cross, near Heathrow Airport. My aim was to spend time with Leslie Brierley, whose research on countries had greatly helped my early work on *Operation World*. I wanted to establish a closer working relationship with him for the future, but I found him recovering from a terrible car accident in Scotland that had killed his wife and a Cuban missionary.

I don't remember everything we discussed, but a key relationship was established. I never dreamed I would one day succeed Leslie in his research role at WEC International.

Jill managed well during our seven months in Europe, despite being pregnant with our honeymoon baby. Her pregnancy caused some embarrassment since she was "showing" so soon after our wedding. Peter was born nine months after our marriage. We were excited and thankful, but we also faced multiple challenges regarding where we would live when we returned to Rhodesia. The main house at the Bible school in Salisbury was only a temporary solution, and with my ongoing work leading teams across that large country, the prospect of frequent separations from Jill and our newborn son was not something I wanted to contemplate.

As we pondered our options, Jill and I decided that purchasing a caravan (known as a camper in America) would enable us to minister together as we traveled around southern Africa. In April 1969, we commenced our second term in Africa, feeling uneasy as the storm clouds of war gathered on the horizon. For nearly four years, our family lived in this 13-foot-long caravan—our wonderful little home. We made some improvements to it and adapted as our family grew. Peter was born three months after we returned to Rhodesia, and he lived in fifty-seven different locations as we traveled around southern Africa holding evangelistic meetings.

Life in our little 13-foot moving home was not easy, but it worked well for our first two boys. It meant that Jill could have a role in the work during those early years of our marriage, and crucially, we were able to be together as a family. I did everything I could to help Jill, cooking meals and washing dirty diapers to give her space to minister. Our coworkers were astonished by how we functioned, as many African men thought it preposterous that a husband would do any menial tasks. We had ample opportunity to live as a couple and as parents in front of our colleagues, and many imitated what we did, in great contrast to what they had seen in their own families.

As we drove to each evangelistic campaign, we must have been quite a sight! Our trusty Mercedes van carried our large tent on the roof, while the team rode inside. Driving over the rough, corrugated African roads damaged my back and caused me much pain over the years, while Jill, being short, had problems driving the van. The seat allowed only minimal adjustment, and her heels could not reach the floor. If she accelerated too quickly, she would lurch backward, causing us to slow down as her foot came off the accelerator. I called it her kangaroo start! I also used the van as my office when I started work on the next edition of *Operation World*.

Peter was born in Salisbury, Rhodesia, but as soon as he was discharged from the hospital, he began to suffer from acute colic and pain. For many months, he cried constantly from early morning to late at night. Jill, who had been a great midwife to countless women and their babies, now felt like a complete failure as a mother. To add insult to injury, some of our teammates began to criticize how "badly" she was managing her baby. Although Jill tried all sorts of remedies, nothing worked. She carried Peter everywhere on her back in a special sling that African mothers use, and the only way she could quiet him was to breastfeed or hold a pacifier in his mouth. If not lightly held in place with a finger, Peter would spit it out after a few minutes when pain spasms hit him.

Once, I had to be away with the team for a month, and in that era—long before the invention of computers and cell phones—the only way Jill and I could communicate was by letter. Reading through those letters years later made me realize what a terribly difficult time Jill went through during that month of separation.

For the next three years, we were hardly ever separated again, as we continued to travel together as a family in our caravan. Those years were very special to us. We became a close-knit family and were able to minister as a married couple with children in a more integrated way than when we were single. Life and ministry in Africa continued to bring painful storms, but Jill was a great peacemaker, smoothing over any emerging conflicts I had with my African colleagues. Team members often told me that Jill had humanized me!

For years we shared many wonderful family experiences, but as any missionary to Africa can attest, living on that great continent comes with challenges, amplified by our nomadic lifestyle. We had to deal with insects—mosquitos, armored cockroaches, and maggots. The latter were particularly unpleasant. Once, a fly laid its eggs on Peter's pillow. They hatched, and the maggots crawled onto his back and scalp, burrowing under his skin and forming dozens of pustules—each containing a maggot. Thankfully, local knowledge came to our aid. We shaved off Peter's hair and smeared him with butter. The butter prevented air from passing through his skin, causing the maggots to suffocate and die.

These intense years established workable ministry patterns for me as I maintained various ministries. I led and participated in team outreach and discipleship, used the afternoons to research and write *Operation World*, and revised Bible text for John's Gospel in the Nambya language. I had to trust God and adapt to being an evangelist, discipler, researcher, and Bible translator—while also being the best husband and father I could be.

Although we were stretched in multiple directions, the Lord Jesus held everything together so we didn't snap! He also encouraged us by regularly doing extraordinary things that displayed his grace and saving power. Once, we held a prayer conference at the beautiful Victoria Falls, attended by many intercessors from South Africa and Rhodesia. A British tourist named Alan was visiting the falls when he saw our large tent. As he walked around it, he was astonished to hear someone praying for God to have mercy on his homeland. Alan turned out to be a backsliding member of my sending church in Liverpool. He was so moved to hear those prayers that he recommitted his life to Jesus and went on to become a pastor in the United Kingdom.

Another great joy was the remarkable conversion of Steve Lungu's mother. Steve's parents had a troubled relationship, and one day, after a huge quarrel, his father walked out of the house never to return. His mother then took Steve and his three siblings to the bus station and told them to wait outside a shop until she returned, but she never did. The children were abandoned and had to fend for themselves. For many years, Steve had no contact with his mother. After becoming a gang leader, his sole ambition was to find his mother and stab her to death, as recorded in his biography, *Out of the Black Shadows*.

We were holding a month of meetings near Salisbury when she came to the tent and went forward for prayer in response to her son's preaching. She was wonderfully converted to Jesus, and her life was transformed. She later attended our Bible school and trained to be an evangelist, serving for many years in her homeland of Zambia, winning people to Christ.

Years later, Steve heard that his father was still alive in a remote village in Malawi. He found him, and his father became a Christian and eventually moved in with Steve's family. His father often said he could not understand how his abandoned son could forgive and welcome him after all the suffering he had caused the family.

11

1974
OPERATION WORLD 2

In 1968, Hans von Staden reminded me that the first little *Operation World* booklet was four years old and needed updating. He asked if I would be willing to revise it and publish a new volume. My response, in retrospect, was audacious in its ignorance! I said that I would gladly revise it, but I would need to expand it to cover the other countries not mentioned in the first edition.

At that stage, I didn't even know how many countries there were in the world, and I had no idea how difficult it would be to fulfill my commitment.

To make matters worse, I was living in a country hemmed in by sanctions imposed by the United Nations. Rhodesia was cut off from the rest of the world, with travel, trade, and even postal services disrupted. I had no office, no access to a good library, and my time was also occupied with leading evangelistic teams. How could I possibly find the time to write?

However, the Lord Jesus loves to take impossible situations and turn them around. From this low starting point—while still adapting to married life with a new baby—I began the process of creating the first global version of *Operation World*. My work on the book had to be squeezed into spare moments, so in the afternoons while my teammates were visiting houses in the townships, I would sit in the back of the van with a portable typewriter on my lap.

I also received vital help from various sources. The 1967 edition of the *World Christian Handbook* by Kenneth Grubb was a great resource. Although it was primarily a listing of the denominations and mission organizations active in each country, it became like a tree trunk for all the other branches of information I began to gather.

Meanwhile, over the next three years, our family continued to travel around southern Africa, building relationships with church leaders and holding tent meetings. Having Jill with me as we travelled was a tremendous asset—among her many gifts, she was a wonderful peacemaker. Often, I would sit in the van beside the tent and work on the book while my colleagues invited people to our evening meetings. My concentration was frequently interrupted by people coming to argue or ask for spiritual counsel, but these interruptions were welcome breaks.

All of this occurred as war clouds gathered over Rhodesia, leading to a contest between the African majority and the incumbent white minority government. It was a time of rising tensions but also of openness to the Gospel, especially among young people.

I was a frontline missionary, driven by a desire to mobilize prayer and recruits to meet the real needs of every country in the world. I deliberately avoided making my books academic in nature, aiming to write in a way that would engage housewives, children, and factory workers in the Great Commission, rather than just scholars and the highly educated.

I was trained as a research scientist and am grateful for the tools this gave me. At the same time, David Barrett, from his missionary base in Kenya, began work on what would become the *World Christian Encyclopedia* a decade later. His intention was to "evangelize" academia through this remarkable work. While he succeeded in this goal, the result was a very expensive volume that adorned the shelves of academic libraries but remained largely inaccessible to ordinary Christians.

Because communication was restricted from my base in Rhodesia, I again contacted Leslie Brierley of WEC at his international research office in England, asking if he could forward letters to church leaders in countries that I was unable to directly contact. Without the wonderful help of Leslie and his team, I doubt I would have been able to complete this project. It must be difficult for someone in the twenty-first century to imagine a world with restricted mail, extremely expensive international phone calls, no internet or email, and few libraries!

As I researched specific countries, many questions arose. So I typed hundreds of letters requesting information that I hoped would fit the expertise of the recipients. I soon discovered that lengthy questionnaires with generic questions did not elicit much response. Each letter needed to be as concise as possible and relevant to the ministry of the informant to avoid overwhelming the recipients.

One important lesson I learned is that research is an ever-changing process. It is better to publish figures that may be slightly inaccurate than to wait for perfection before publishing something—perfection is unobtainable in a fluid, imperfect world. I believed that by publishing the best information I had at the time, others could later improve on my work, creating more accurate future editions.

Another development that helped the process move forward was the gradual establishment of a network of informants around the world. Many of these individuals not only provided invaluable information but also became friends and were a vital resource for correcting and preparing new editions. I am deeply grateful to the many people who responded to an unknown person in a remote land and were willing to contribute to an unproven project.

Like a rolling snowball, the first global *Operation World* slowly gained momentum. With each passing day, I grew slightly more confident that I would eventually see light at the end of the tunnel and that a quality resource would emerge to aid the task of world evangelization.

During the process, I developed some God-given principles that served me well for decades. For instance, I learned to engage with readers who criticized my books by inviting them to become helpers. Most complaints arose because I included groups or denominations that some considered unworthy of inclusion. Readers didn't understand that including a marginal group in a list of a country's religious affiliations did not mean that I endorsed their beliefs or practices. My intention was to give an inclusive and complete picture and let my readers evaluate how to handle the information. By responding warmly, thanking critics for their input, and inviting them to help with the next edition, many critics became my allies!

As the project continued to take shape, I began to explore publishing options. During this time, Kees and Else Lugthart from the Netherlands joined the Dorothea Mission and set up a printing press at the Pretoria base, primarily to produce evangelistic literature. Kees had a huge typesetting machine on which he retyped the text to create lead blocks of print—something hard to comprehend in our digitized world today! Hans von Staden asked him to print the first global *Operation World*. As he progressed with the typesetting, his walls became lined with blocks of lead type and completed pages, and then he printed the books on his Heidelberg press.

Only after Kees had painstakingly typeset the book, printed the two hundred pages, and collated them by hand did we discover that, according to South African law, no book could be marketed commercially unless it was printed in a shop staffed by members of the powerful printers' trade union. We faced a disaster because we could not legally sell the book! To sidestep this restriction, we printed 3,000 copies for use in our weekly intercession meetings, all of which were given away free of charge to avoid legal problems. I also sent complimentary copies to all the main contributors to the book.

Although the process had been long and complicated, it was a relief to finally have the second edition (and first global version) of *Operation World* in print and circulating. I had begun work on it in 1968, and six long years had elapsed before the project finally reached its fulfillment in 1974.

The first global *Operation World* featured several innovations. Among them was that I applied a 100 percent rule for religions so that all countries would have a complete breakdown of their population's religious affiliation by percentage. I could not find any other book that fully enumerated this crucial demographic. Most publications offered generic statements, such as, "The dominant religion of Morocco is Islam." In contrast, we provided a statistical breakdown showing how many people in each country were Muslims, Christians, Buddhists, Jews, or adherents of other major religions.

I also sought a way to enumerate evangelical Christians so that people could easily gauge the "reachedness" of a country. At the time, we didn't have a clear definition of what an evangelical was or how to count them. I made my own estimates of the number of "born again believers" based on each denomination's size, its theological stance on the Bible, and the possible proportion of active members who might have a living faith. I then applied the same criteria to each country in the world. This approach provided a reasonable assessment of the level of Bible-based Christianity in each country, and it was the best we could do at the time.

In later editions, *Operation World* defined evangelicals as those who recognize these four main attributes of the faith: that the Lord Jesus Christ is the sole source of salvation through faith in him; that personal faith and conversion are experienced with regeneration by the Holy Spirit; that the Bible is the inspired Word of God and the only basis for faith and Christian living; and that commitment to biblical witness, evangelism, and mission brings others to faith in Christ.

We also developed a rule that we would always count individuals according to what they claimed to be. For instance, if a person identified as Muslim, Christian, or non-religious in a poll or census, that is how we counted them—even if they were nominal, sectarian, or backsliding. Our statistics were therefore based on profession of faith. If someone claimed to be a Christian, we counted them accordingly, even though the number of truly born-again believers may have been considerably lower.

Over the years, other Christian researchers and I came to see that counting people by their own profession of faith is really the only way to compile useful data. How could we accurately measure the number of people who have really come to new life in Christ? Many people have asked me over the years for a figure on the number of "born-again" Christians in a country, and I have jokingly replied that I have never been given permission to peek into the Lamb's Book of Life—a book that has yet to be opened! We needed a more objective mechanism.

The true number of believers who have appropriated the saving grace of God and passed from death to life, can ultimately only be quantified by the Great Researcher, for "The Lord knows those who are his" (2 Tim 2:19). In places where widespread nominalism has blighted the Christian population, I often joked: "It is very hard to mobilize unconverted pastors to mobilize their unconverted membership to go out and evangelize the unconverted!" To me, nominal Christianity underlined the importance of knowing the size of the "mobilizable" population of believers in a country, and I sought ways to estimate and express that number.

Hans von Staden wrote a foreword for the book, closing with these words: "Surely some great publishing house will discover the potential of this book and make a wide circulation possible through the trade." I sent a copy of the book to Moody Press in Chicago. They responded that they had looked long and hard at the book but decided it was unmarketable. Years later, I spoke with one of the leaders of Moody Press, who told me that this was probably the biggest publishing mistake they had ever made!

I also sent a copy to Ralph Winter, who had recently bought the property in Pasadena, California, that became the US Center for World Mission. As part of his vision, a monthly magazine,

Mission Frontiers, and a publishing arm, William Carey Library, were also launched on site. Ralph was enthusiastic, having never seen a book like *Operation World* before. He recognized its potential to become a valuable resource for mobilizing prayer and recruits for the frontier peoples of the world on which the Center was focused. He wrote back to us asking if they could publish the book. William Carey Library released their edition in 1976, under the title *The World Handbook for the World Christian*.

Winter annoyed me by including several of his own articles in an appendix. I was not consulted about the cumbersome title or some of the articles—which included parts I disagreed with! Foolishly, no contract was drawn up for the book, so no arrangements existed regarding the conditions of sale or payment of royalties. I had much to learn about the painful challenge of negotiating with publishers.

12

Banishment

The first three years Jill and I spent back in Africa were nomadic, traveling the length and breadth of Rhodesia in our little caravan, with forays into Botswana and South Africa. Jill was able to juggle being an excellent mother with her involvement on the ministry teams.

Two years after Peter's birth, our second son, Timothy, arrived. He was a happy, placid baby—the very opposite of his brother! Timothy was so relaxed that even while he was still in the womb, Jill frequently asked me to listen for a heartbeat to ensure he was alive. We had thought our second child would be a girl and had already chosen a name for her—Ruth. Ruth did eventually arrive 18 months later, making us a family of five.

Living with two toddlers in a 13-foot caravan worked for us, but when Ruth was on the way, we knew we had to adjust our lifestyle and find a more permanent home. Peter would soon need to start school, and a more stable environment would be needed. In June 1972, a crisis occurred that expedited our plans. Both Jill and Tim fell seriously ill with glandular fever, with Tim developing an extraordinary rash of large, coin-sized spots all over his body. I had to rush them back to our base in Salisbury, not realizing that Jill was already pregnant with Ruth. We thank the Lord that the illness had no adverse effect on our unborn baby!

Jill had always said she would give full attention to the children until they started school, at which time she hoped to have more freedom to re-engage in ministry. Having three little ones in less than four years proved to be a full-time job. Thinking it would be ideal if we found a property near our Bible school in Salisbury, so we could be involved with the students, I wrote a letter proposing this plan to our South African head office.

Expecting our leaders to see the urgency of our need, we were surprised when months passed without a response. We continued to travel and hold campaigns, and later that year, while ministering in the city of Gweru, two members of the Dorothea Mission council arrived unannounced from South Africa. Before reaching Gweru, they had visited Bulawayo, the second-largest city in Rhodesia, and rented a second-floor apartment for us. Only then did they inform us that the ministry had "fixed" our accommodation problem—without any consultation at all. Their unilateral action left us deeply disturbed and dismayed.

The pain caused by their actions can hardly be described. The fact that they had secretly concocted this plan without any hint of their thinking or discussion left us feeling bewildered and disrespected. Here we were, leading the evangelistic work in the country, yet we were not considered worthy of being involved in a discussion about our family's needs and location.

Salisbury was where most of our African coworkers lived and the location of our mission's Bible school. Moving to Bulawayo would effectively mean Jill's banishment from any ministry involvement with the mission to which God had called us. While Salisbury (now Harare) was conveniently situated in the north-central part of the country with easy access to other large population centers, Bulawayo was 270 miles (440 km) away in southern Rhodesia. The long distances from most of the towns where we held our tent campaigns meant I would be separated from Jill and the children for eight or nine months each year.

Being based in Bulawayo would also mean greatly increased travel and other costs between each campaign. At the time, fuel rationing in Rhodesia had become increasingly severe because of sanctions. We were allowed coupons to purchase just sixteen gallons of diesel fuel every month. This was enough to drive to a distant location for a tent campaign, but then we'd have to wait for the next month's allocation to return home. Neither was it enough to travel from Bulawayo to Salisbury to pick up our tent and workers. We lived on a shoestring budget, with very little support coming in locally or from overseas, and we rarely received anything from our head office in South Africa. We had been just scraping by, barely able to pay our workers' monthly allowances, and now we had to bear the additional costs of increased travel and rent for an inappropriate apartment.

Although we spent hours trying to reason with the Dorothea leaders, we were left with no alternative but to reluctantly agree to the move. We requested just one condition—that the rent be paid directly to the owners from South Africa. This was agreed to but never done. The stress in our lives suddenly escalated. I had enough obstacles each day as I wrestled with finishing the second edition of *Operation World*, and these unwelcome stresses imposed by our own ministry leaders almost broke me.

Arriving in unfamiliar Bulawayo to a barren apartment, Jill and I had to immediately find a fridge, cooker, washing machine, and furniture. We also needed a parking space for our caravan. Our apartment was two floors above ground and proved to be dangerous for our family. We almost lost Tim, who climbed onto the window ledge; his life was only spared because Peter grabbed him by his trousers just as he was about to fall out.

Over the following years, I repeatedly asked Hans von Staden to explain the mission's extraordinary decision to relocate us without consultation. His inability to respond led us to draw our own conclusions, which were confirmed years later by a subsequent leader of the mission. Jill enjoyed such close relationships with the African workers that she became a threat to one of our local mission leaders, prompting them to organize our relocation to a distant city, even if it meant disruption to our ministry and separation from our team members still based in Salisbury.

Despite the obstacles, the Lord Jesus continued to miraculously provide for us and our coworkers. Once, we held a tent campaign in the neighboring country of Botswana. We had enough money to drive the hundreds of miles across the Kalahari Desert to our destination, but not enough to return home. I was able to leave Jill only a few dollars to take care of the children. But I had completely forgotten about the monthly rent of $80, and while I was away, the bill arrived, and Jill could not pay it. After she prayed, she received an unusual phone call from a distraught woman who had married a man she later discovered was already married to another woman. She sought advice from local pastors, but none would make the time to meet with her. Jill gladly spent time counseling and praying with her. To show her appreciation, at the end of their time together, she handed Jill an envelope containing $100, which allowed Jill to pay the rent and buy food.

On another occasion, while I was away, Jill became ill with influenza, and a Christian friend stopped by for a visit. Seeing Jill's condition, she offered to go across the road to get some aspirin at a local pharmacy. Jill had no choice but to admit she was penniless and could not afford it. The friend was so upset that she went straight to Brian and Muriel Russell, the leaders of the Baptist Church where we were members. Within a few hours, the Russells arrived at our door, demanding to know the reasons for our dire poverty. From that point on, they added us to their list of supported missionaries.

By the end of our second term in June 1974, five of our African team members had married, and two more were engaged. They had first come to us as single men and women, and we had watched as the Holy Spirit refined these rough diamonds into polished gemstones that reflected his glory. Now they were mature believers and excellent ministers of the gospel.

Over time, team relationships steadily improved as we all matured, and teammates became dear friends, not merely coworkers. We still had occasional disputes, but they were fewer and less intense. We truly were like a big family, sharing both good and bad times together as we journeyed through life. And like a family, we helped each other in practical ways. I taught some of our coworkers how to drive and helped them obtain licenses. I also introduced some to the basics of accounting.

Steve Lungu found Rachel, a lovely, well-educated Malawian from a good family. She brought great stability to Steve, who had never experienced a healthy family environment. Josias Ngara, one of our blind workers, found Dorothy, who was also blind and a teacher. Both were talented individuals who managed life well together with their subsequent sighted children.

Two teammates, Gibson and Maggie, faced the challenges of a cross-cultural marriage. Maggie was from the Ndebele tribe, and Gibson was a Manyika Shona, with their families located at opposite ends of the country. One weekend, we all drove across Rhodesia for their wedding at a Methodist church near Mutare.

Gibson's older brother, a local chief who had once been a church elder, had backslidden and been disciplined for polygamy and drunkenness. We stayed in his home and pleaded with him not to drink any alcohol before the wedding ceremony. However, on the morning of the big day, he disappeared and eventually turned up reeking of alcohol but seemingly in his right mind.

By the time we reached the church, the alcohol had taken its effect. In his stupefied state, he sat down on one of the benches where the church leaders usually sat. As I was the preacher that day, I was seated next to him. When the service began, he gradually nodded off into a drunken slumber. After several big nods and recoveries, his head dropped down to his knees, snapping his jaw shut and locking his teeth onto a fold in his trousers. He fell forward, ripping his trousers open with his teeth as he collapsed on the floor. By this time, everyone was deeply embarrassed, and Maggie, the bride, was in tears. The ceremony proceeded, and I preached with him lying fast asleep on the floor. It was a wedding day remembered for all the wrong reasons, but Maggie and Gibson continued to faithfully serve God and were later appointed leaders of the Dorothea Mission in Zimbabwe.

We also found time to expand our work into Botswana and Mozambique, which led to some funny cultural misunderstandings for our team. In Botswana, none of us spoke Tswana, the national language, and the culture was strangely incoherent to our African coworkers. Chipo, one of our members, was offered some eggs by a group of Tswana mothers. In response, Chipo did the usual Shona gesture of showing appreciation by slowly clapping her hands together, which is often done instead of saying "thank you." To Chipo's astonishment, the Tswana ladies withdrew without handing over the eggs. We later learned that clapping hands means "No, thank you" in Tswana culture!

The last year of our second term in Africa was fruitful, so we had lots to share when we visited European and British churches. We also had something to eagerly look forward to. Shortly before we left for England, a missionary friend told us they would be permanently leaving Rhodesia during our time away. Their home was in an ideal location and much better suited to our family's needs, so we planned to move into our "dream house" upon our return to Africa.

When we were married in 1968, Jill and I enjoyed a brief honeymoon in the Lake District before we hurried off for ministry in Europe. Much had changed, and by our second home leave in September 1974, we had three children in tow. June, Jill's twin sister, kindly took the children, allowing us to enjoy another week in the Lake District to complete our honeymoon!

As we reflected on our second term in Africa, Jill and I realized we had constantly battled to keep our relationship strong due to our long and frequent separations, exacerbated by our ministry banishing us to isolated Bulawayo. Jill gradually developed her own contacts and ministry outside the home, and occasionally I would turn up exhausted and with the expectation of rest and loving care.

I'm afraid I had become little more than a disruptor of our family's routines and responsibilities. Many household chores and repairs were neglected, which Jill rightfully expected her husband to do. Those years were hard on us, as our time apart meant that neither of us could adequately meet the other's needs. I needed to radically adjust my ministry activities.

13

1978—
OPERATION WORLD 3

We arrived back in Rhodesia in February 1975 and moved into our new rented home in Bulawayo, which became a very special place for our family. Peter attended an excellent school nearby, and for the first time in years, we had a stable environment to thrive in.

The property had a good-sized garden, which was a happy and safe place for our children to play in. We grew sixteen different varieties of fruit, including mango, guava, lemon, orange, tangerine, pawpaw, fig, avocado, mulberry, peach, passionfruit, and apples. Since then, I have been a jam maker, producing large quantities of jams and jellies each year.

By God's grace and through the love of many friends, our financial situation improved, and we received a growing number of unsolicited gifts that covered 70 percent of our ministry expenses, including personal allowances for all our team members.

The year 1974 was also significant due to the Congress on World Evangelization held in Lausanne, Switzerland, where more than 2,300 evangelical leaders from 150 countries gathered. At that time, my ministry and writing had not yet gained enough prominence for me to be invited. I would have loved to have been there—particularly for the seminal address by Ralph Winter, which electrified the Congress with his call to go and disciple the 16,750 "hidden" people groups of the world. This address shifted the focus of Christian activity from broadly ministering to entire countries to specifically targeting the ethnic and linguistic groups within and beyond those borders, marking a major realignment of missionary strategy and deployment.

When Winter was asked for information or a list of those peoples, he could not provide one, for none yet existed; his specific total was a statistical estimate based on limited data. Identifying, mapping, and profiling the people groups of the world became the great new thrust of Christian research from the 1980s to the present.

The impact of this recalibration of vision in the mission world has been huge. Since the Lausanne Conference, Christians have been looking at the task of world evangelization more as God sees it, with the ultimate goal of making disciples among "every nation, tribe, people, and language" (Rev 7:9).

In my own country of ministry, Rhodesia (now Zimbabwe), there are over forty ethnic groups speaking twenty-three distinct languages. These range from the large Shona groups, containing millions of people, to smaller tribes, such as the 127,000 Nambya people, with whom I was blessed to participate in translating of parts of the New Testament. Each group required a fresh strategy and emphasis to effectively reach and disciple them for Jesus Christ. This sharper focus, repeated across the globe, has transformed the mission world over the past half-century.

As our family returned to Africa for our third term, our work was overshadowed by growing opposition to the white minority governments in southern Africa and by escalating violence or wars in Mozambique, Angola, Namibia, and Rhodesia. The Communists were also on the march, creating a general sense that they were succeeding in their aim for world domination.

We were able to obtain a small Renault 5 car shortly after our return, which became a vital part of Jill's life, especially given the strict fuel rationing of just six gallons per month. The car made life so much easier for Jill when I was away and later when I handed over our van to the team. It opened many doors of ministry for Jill, and God connected her with people from all racial backgrounds who were in both physical and spiritual need.

At the end of 1975, we hosted a visit from my mother and stepfather, during which they met many of our Christian friends. When my mother attended a tent campaign in Bulawayo one night, it provided her with a glimpse into the ministry to which I had dedicated my life, potentially shaking her long-held belief that I had wasted my university qualifications. In retrospect, this was the last year we could have welcomed them to our home. From 1976 onward, the guerrilla war escalated sharply, and few tourists entered the country.

Over the previous decade, Russia and other Communist bloc countries flooded the region with finance, personnel, and weapons. Meanwhile, an insurgent group led by Robert Mugabe set up camps in Mozambique to train freedom fighters to liberate Rhodesia. Their influence quickly spread, ultimately leading to their takeover of the country. Rhodesia was renamed Zimbabwe in 1980, and Mugabe led the country for thirty-seven years until 2017. In Mozambique, Frelimo insurgents fought a devastating war against the Portuguese colonial authorities, which ended in 1975 with the collapse of the dictatorship in Portugal and the rapid handover of their colonial possessions to Marxist insurgents. The independence gained in 1975 bolstered the Zimbabwean insurgents based in Mozambique. Although the region was gradually descending into violence, we knew that, as servants of Christ, the chaos presented opportunities to share the gospel with more people. Consequently, I traveled into the tumultuous environment of Mozambique to explore potential ministry opportunities with Steve Lungu and a South African missionary friend.

We arrived in the city of Beira during the transition to a Marxist government. We managed to interview the new governor and were delighted when he granted us permission to return and hold a tent campaign in the city. However, both the outgoing Portuguese authorities and the governor later advised against our plans because of the danger of violence. The following year, Steve led a team to Mozambique for a month. They were arrested and imprisoned for a short while, until a policeman who had attended one of their meetings spoke up for them and won their release.

Shortly after our visit, the Frelimo Marxists began dismantling Mozambique's colonial structures, imposing Communism more forcefully, and ordering the expulsion of 200,000 ethnic Portuguese. A full-blown civil war ensued, lasting for fifteen years and concluding in 1992. Mozambique then shed its Marxist ideology, adopted a market economy, embraced a measure of democracy, and even joined the British Commonwealth in 1995.

As the political and military situation became increasingly unstable, Jill and I wondered what the future held for us. We continued to hold meetings for the next year, and in the African townships, I still felt free. My knowledge of local languages helped alleviate suspicions, although people increasingly asked what "this white man" was doing. The greater dangers occurred when we traveled on remote unpaved roads, which were more susceptible to landmines often hidden in tree shadows or under puddles.

As the situation deteriorated, it became clear that the era of white missionary work in Rhodesia was rapidly drawing to a close. Within eighteen months, a series of crises arose that changed everything and hastened the handover of the work to my African colleagues, allowing the ministry to continue without foreign oversight. That final year and a half of team ministry proved to be redemptive in many ways. Our ministry produced considerable fruit, and it was a joy to return to areas and find new believers from previous campaigns still walking with Jesus.

Communist ideology was spreading in the townships, and increasingly prepared believers for coming persecution. I wrote two booklets on coping with persecution, which were translated into Ndebele and Shona. We chose plain covers for these booklets in the hope that when persecution came, the literature would not be considered subversive. When Marxism was imposed a few years later, most Christians were strong enough to resist attempts to suppress church and ministry life, and there was never a time of real persecution.

As society in southern Africa seemed to lurch ever closer to a precipice, I continued to research and write country profiles in preparation for the next edition of *Operation World* from the moment we returned to Rhodesia in 1975. When I had completed the first global edition several years earlier, I sent a copy to George Verwer, the founding leader of Operation Mobilization (OM). At that time, OM was a mission filled with enthusiastic young people who were courageous witnesses for Jesus. George had written to me, offering to publish *Operation World* if I wrote a third edition. George now contacted me again, as literature had become a major focus of his ministry, and he had recently set up a publishing arm called Send the Light. I took up his offer and worked closely with his team.

Throughout 1975, I reactivated my network of information sources around the world and added others to my list. The concept of editing text on a computer and sending emails was still two decades away, so communication had to be done by letter, using carbon copies for files. Every outgoing letter had to be crafted to maximize the chance of gaining some positive information. We had to be patient, as a response could take months—if there was a response at all. I again relied on my intermediary helpers, especially my friends at the WEC headquarters in England, to send letters to countries that would not accept mail from Rhodesia.

This time, I had a proper contract and a respected Christian publisher. Since the third *Operation World* was likely to have a worldwide reach, I rearranged the text from its African orientation to a global one. The information and prayer items were framed in terms of a likely lifespan of five years. We avoided prayer requests for specific events that could make the book appear obsolete. I also rarely used the names of political or religious leaders in the prayer sections of each country, as the world was changing rapidly, and the book was likely to outlast their tenure in office.

It took me three years to complete the new book, which was finally published in 1978. Interest had already been generated, and the book was translated into Afrikaans, Portuguese, German, and Spanish.

As a first-time author with Send the Light, I was ignorant about all the twists and turns involved in book negotiations. I was persuaded to accept a royalty of just 2 percent on net sales for our mission. I was told that the risks of publishing such a book were so high that two percent was adequate compensation. In reality, such a low royalty level didn't even come close to covering our costs, personally or as a mission, to bring this third edition to publication. Thankfully, I did not write books to make money but to impact the kingdom of God, and he made it a success!

I never kept statistics on how many copies were printed of each *Operation World*, but I remember that this edition sold between 250,000 and 300,000 copies in the 1978 and 1979 printings, plus smaller print runs in the other language editions.

It was a great blessing to know that what had started as a little prayer booklet for a few thousand intercessors in 1964 had grown to a book that hundreds of thousands of Christians around the world were regularly using. This was all the doing of the Lord, and I was just glad that the name of Jesus was being glorified, and his kingdom was expanding.

14

Out of Africa

In February and March 1976, while we were running a campaign in Fort Victoria (Masvingo), distressing news arrived from Jill in Bulawayo. Our little Renault had been vandalized, and the lock in our driveway was damaged. Many vagrants were using our garden as an escape route, leaving Jill and our three children vulnerable and exposed to violence. At that moment, I instinctively knew that our time in Rhodesia was nearing its end and that a full leadership handover had to be completed soon.

I wrote to Hans von Staden, detailing the worsening situation and outlining some options for how we might fit into future ministry plans. Hans was a man of great vision, faith, and prayer, but after experiencing many hard knocks in life and disappointments with potential leaders, he found it hard to let go of control.

Consequently, any thoughts Jill and I might have had about taking on a leadership role in the Dorothea Mission were out of the question. Once, when challenged by another mission leader to find a successor to whom he could hand over the ministry, Hans responded, "No, I will not hand over. I will die as the leader." His health was always fragile, but he managed to hold on until his death several years later. Sadly, much of the ministry's vision and dynamism died with him.

As Jill and I began actively praying about our future ministry, our primary concern was that our African team members would function well after we were gone. We were also worried that if we unduly prolonged our leadership of the team, we would hinder their growth in ministry.

In early 1977, I received an invitation to speak at a conference in Germany for four hundred Bible school students from across Europe. The von Stadens agreed that I should go, and I traveled to Germany for two weeks of meetings. This trip proved to be a strategic door opener for our future service to God.

Firstly, I met Traugott Boeker, a WEC missionary waiting for a visa to serve in Indonesia. He became the first translator of *Operation World* into German. He had just completed that task and at last was granted the coveted but long-delayed visa!

Secondly, I met Operation Mobilization European leaders with whom I found an immediate bond. They asked me to come to Switzerland for several days after the conference, and this cemented my relationship with them and contributed to our involvement with the ministry of the MV Logos for a year of ministry two years later.

Thirdly, I was offered a ministry to be in charge of a Christian research office. After the conference and some ministry in Germany, I arranged to spend a few days with my parents. My mother took me to Heathrow Airport a bit early because of another visit she needed to make. So, I used the extra hours to phone Leslie Brierley of WEC at the WEC headquarters just ten miles from Heathrow. He answered immediately and said, "I have been trying to track you down! Can I come to the airport right now for a chat?" To my surprise, Leslie brought along Alastair Kennedy, the deputy director of WEC. We enjoyed such great fellowship that I almost missed my flight back to Africa! As I boarded my plane, Leslie casually said, "My research desk at WEC will soon be empty. How about you take it over?" I laughed and replied, "I haven't had a word from the Lord about that!"

Soon after my return to Rhodesia, I was driving on a country road when the Lord suddenly spoke: "You will never travel on this road again!" Whether the voice was audible or in my spirit, I could not tell, but it scarcely mattered, for it was so clear and forceful that I broke out into a cold sweat, contemplating what this would mean for our family.

A short time later, we received a letter from Leslie Brierley, asking if Jill and I would be open for WEC to approach the Dorothea Mission with a view to my taking over as the director of research for WEC. With the recent word from the Lord ringing in my ears, I forwarded the letter to Hans von Staden, who responded cautiously but positively. I think he realized that with *Operation World* and my global connections developing as they were, my ministry would be limited if I remained within the sphere of the Dorothea Mission. Things moved quickly after that. Leslie invited me to a WEC conference in Scotland in May 1978, allowing me to meet the entire global leadership team of WEC. This allowed them a chance to interview me and gave me a chance to observe WEC and get to know many of the mission leaders from around the world.

After visiting my mother and stepfather, I traveled north from Bristol to Scotland and was surprised to discover that I was on the same train and in the same carriage as Helen Roseveare, a well-known WEC missionary-doctor who had written many books about her dramatic experiences during the civil war in Congo. She was imprisoned by rebel forces in 1964 and subjected to beatings and rape, but she astonished many by returning to the Congo to help rebuild the nation, including reconstructing hospitals that had been destroyed in the conflict. Helen and I spent much of the journey sharing about our experiences in Africa and in the Lord.

The conference went extremely well. I was warmly received, although some WEC workers understandably had serious doubts about inviting someone from outside the mission into a top leadership position. One senior missionary was speaking with Leslie and me in one of the conference rooms when he asked outright, "Who is this fellow Johnstone that is being invited to join our mission?" He was deeply embarrassed when he found that "this fellow" was sitting right in front of him. I had an advantage in that I had read most of the books written by Norman Grubb about the background and vision of WEC, and I already loved the spiritual culture and ethos of the ministry.

The World Evangelization Crusade was founded by C. T. Studd, who came from a wealthy family. He shocked British society by rejecting his privileged life as a famous cricket player for England to become a missionary to China with the China Inland Mission in 1885, joining the ranks of the "Cambridge Seven." After serving more than twenty years in China and India, Studd's health deteriorated. He returned to Britain in 1906 as a broken man, and someone who heard Studd speak described him as a "museum of diseases." One night, he was captivated by an advertisement for a church meeting that said, "Cannibals want Missionaries." He attended the service and was deeply touched by the missionary's description of thousands of African villages in Central Africa still waiting to hear the Good news of Jesus Christ for the first time.

Against medical advice and without any support or money, C. T. Studd reasoned that the living God would take care of him if he put his kingdom first. He sailed alone to Africa in 1910, leaving his sick wife to become an advocate for the new mission in the UK. The ministry he founded was first named Heart of Africa Mission. While surveying the unevangelized Sudan region of Darfur, God spoke to him that the new ministry would be for the whole unevangelized world, so it was then launched as Worldwide Evangelization Crusade. It is now known as WEC International.

Apart from the extraordinarily rich spiritual heritage at WEC, I appreciated their servant leadership style, the autonomy of teams in each field to make consensual decisions, and, above all, their vision to reach the most unreached countries and peoples of the world. At the conference, I watched with wonder and admiration as the WEC leaders engaged in robust yet gracious debate, which would never have been allowed in the benign dictatorship of the Dorothea Mission.

Later in the conference, I was interviewed by the inner core of WEC leaders. I recall few of the questions they asked, but the interview went extremely well. They all had a strong sense that God was involved in this unorthodox process of inviting an outsider from another agency to fill one of their four top leadership positions. Since no one receives a salary in WEC, and all are considered volunteers who trust God for their needs, there was no financial motive involved. In fact, during the interview, some jokes were made about the "massive increase" in salary offered to me, from nothing to nothing!

On my final day in Scotland, I sat quietly in my chair, communing with the Lord. In my heart, I had a sense of peace and God's leading, but was I deceived? I remembered how God had initially spoken to me nearly twenty years earlier in my room in Bristol, saying, "I will give you the ends of the earth as your possession." In Africa, as one of those ends, I knew I was fulfilling that vision, but the WEC role meant we would need to relocate back to England, which seemed like a major step backward from the direction our lives had been heading.

As I pondered my call, these words came to my mind: "I have given you *one* end of the earth, but now I will give you the other ends as well!" That settled the matter in my heart, and I returned to Jill and our children with confidence that God was directing us to leave the Dorothea Mission and our beloved Africa.

The WEC leaders wisely asked Hans von Staden if he would agree to an arrangement where the Dorothea Mission would essentially second me to WEC for a two-year period. I was sure that when we finally joined WEC, it would prove to be a permanent move, but I am grateful for the sensitivity they displayed by handling this as a temporary assignment in case things didn't work out. It was a significant risk for WEC to invite someone from outside their organization into their core leadership team.

When I returned to Rhodesia, Jill and I faced the painful task of breaking the news of our pending departure to our African colleagues. At an appropriate moment, I shared what we believed to be God's leading, and everyone was very distressed. Although they were managing well in their evangelistic work, they still saw us as their advocates and protectors in their interactions with the white authorities and with the leaders of the Dorothea Mission, where old paternalistic patterns were slow to change. The team members hardly spoke to me for several days as they processed the painful news.

Jill and I devised a plan to leave Africa a year later, giving plenty of time for a full handover and for packing or disposing of all we had in Africa. However, our timetable proved to be out of sync with God's schedule!

During the conference I attended in Germany in early 1977, I met several Operation Mobilization leaders and was invited to an OM leaders conference in Switzerland, which we traveled to by road. Lasting friendships were formed, including one with Dave Hicks, who at the time was the director of the OM ship, the *MV Logos*. Dave had made use of my emerging manuscript for the new *Operation World* by creating prayer cards that featured basic facts about a country on one side and five or six key prayer points on the other. It was a brilliant idea, and hundreds of thousands of those cards were subsequently distributed in multiple languages as a complement to the third edition as well as to later editions of the book.

A few months later, the *MV Logos* arrived in West Africa with Dave and Cathy Hicks on board. The ship made its way south, visiting several ports in different countries. Dave asked if I would minister on the ship when it docked in Cape Town and Durban, as well as to the 135 crew members during the five-day voyage between the cities.

Those two weeks went well, and on my final day, Dave asked me to walk with him around the port area of Durban. After sharing his vision for the ship ministry, he surprised me by asking if I would consider bringing my family on the ship for a year while I served in a pastoral role to the OM crew members. I laughed and told him that I would need to hear a word from the Lord for such a dramatic change. When I returned to Bulawayo and shared this with Jill, we didn't take Dave's offer seriously because we couldn't see how it lined up with our calling from God, our deep involvement in Africa, and the likely transfer to a global ministry with WEC.

A few weeks after agreeing to join WEC as their director of research, I received a second letter from Dave Hicks on the *MV Logos*, which was then docked in South Korea. He repeated his request that we prayerfully consider spending a year ministering on the ship as part of the OM team. He was unaware of our plans to join WEC, but Jill and I agreed to set aside our own desires and seek the Lord's will concerning this invitation. We brought our young children into the discussion—Peter, who was then 8 years old, Tim, 6, and Ruth, 5. We wanted them to be part of the decision since it would be a radical and life-changing choice for them as well. We all prayed together, and at first, Peter was strongly opposed because he loved Rhodesia and his school, but he gradually warmed to the idea. Tim summed it up well in one prayer when he said, "Lord Jesus, thank you for calling us to be on the ship. You have called Mom and Dad, so we know you have called us too!"

We proposed to the von Stadens that we accelerate our departure by six months, and we asked WEC if we could delay our arrival in the UK by six months. Both ministries agreed, so we expedited our preparations for leaving Africa. We ended up shipping just four trunks of possessions to England, along with our essential library of books, which were mailed in multiple parcels. Everything else, including all our furniture, was either sold or given away—primarily to our colleagues. We sold our caravan and car and found new homes for our dog and cat.

It astonished us that, even though we had struggled financially for much of our time in Africa, on the day of our departure, all our expenses and debts had been paid in full, allowances to our African workers were given, and our five airline tickets were paid for. We even had $1,030 in cash left—just over the legal cash limit the Rhodesian authorities would permit. Our loving Heavenly Father had perfectly sorted out our finances!

We said goodbye to our coworkers and friends at Salisbury Airport with many tears flowing down all our cheeks. As our plane lifted off the runway, I looked out the window at a great pillar of smoke rising from the blaze of a large fuel storage depot that had been bombed by insurgents the day before our departure. The fierce fire and ominous black smoke over the city seemed to signal the conclusion on our time in Rhodesia. We had poured our lives into Africa, and although the future of that nation looked bleak, we knew the Lord Jesus would sustain our brothers and sisters, who were now mature and faithful leaders in the kingdom of God.

Our plane stopped in Pretoria, where we disembarked and made our way to the von Stadens' home. It was an emotional visit. The little Dorothea Mission, despite all its faults and foibles, had been God's instrument in shaping Jill and me into the people he wanted us to be. Although there were times when we wished we were somewhere else, we persevered at the mission through many peaks and valleys. I remain deeply grateful for those sixteen formative years.

15

LIFE ON THE OCEAN WAVES

The ship that would become our home for the next year was docked in Bombay (now Mumbai), India. We arrived in the vast city on a muggy night and were met by several OM workers who transported us to their local base. We stayed there for a few days while the *MV Logos* was at anchor and less accessible, giving us the opportunity to gain some exposure to life in India. What a change from Africa! While we encountered poverty in Africa, India's poverty was on another level and greatly shocked us.

It was a sobering experience to step over little babies lying asleep on the sidewalk, covered only with a cloth, while their parents eked out a living by sorting through piles of trash. The persistent begging by children tugging at our sleeves was also unnerving. Little Ruth, who was six at the time, still has vivid memories of that initial exposure to life in India.

We boarded the 2,300-ton *Logos* and began what would become one of the most exciting and arduous years for the Johnstone family. The daily experiences left indelible marks on our lives.

The *MV Logos* was the fulfilment of a dream of George Verwer, the founder and leader of Operation Mobilization. It seemed like a crazy idea for a young mission to operate a ship, and some critics suggested it should have been named "George's Folly"! The ship had originally been used by the Danish government to haul supplies to remote settlements in Greenland. It had a strong hull to withstand ice floes but inadequate air conditioning for life in the tropics. How we sweltered in those cabins!

The *Logos* was the first of what later became a small navy of Christian ships serving people around the world, including the Mercy Ships of Youth With A Mission (YWAM). With George's passion for promoting and distributing Christian literature, the focus of the ship's ministry revolved around its floating book exhibition on the foredeck, featuring vast quantities of educational and Christian literature for the masses who came aboard at each port of call. Over the years, millions of Bibles and other Christian books were sold or given away to visitors of the OM ships.

Looking back, I marvel at what has been achieved through the ministries of evangelism, literature, and discipleship for visitors and crew on these gospel ships. From among the thousands of OM "graduates," countless leaders, pastors, and pioneers have emerged. Many indigenous mission organizations and churches today are led by OM graduates. Some of the godly men and women I came to know on the *Logos* became close friends in the years that followed. They were great conduits of information and advice for later editions of *Operation World*.

Life on the ship impacted each of our family members, making it a very special experience for our children. There were two schoolteachers on board who gave the small group of children almost individual attention. Geography lessons came alive as we visited eleven countries in twelve months.

Our family was housed in a small double cabin with three beds and the floor serving as a play area for the children. Jill and I slept on a bunk bed in the main cabin, which transformed into a couch during the day. We were next to the scullery, where all the galley cooking pots were stored, so when the seas were rough, the banging and clashing of the pots kept us awake.

Life on board was extremely busy. In addition to the daily work of maintaining and running the ship and feeding and caring for the crew, we ministered to thousands of visitors at each port of call. We were in a constant state of exhaustion due to the noise, close quarters, and the never-ending work and ministry, but we loved it! Jill and I were involved in leading morning devotions and evening prayer meetings, and in encouraging and discipling crew members.

While in port, we often hosted conferences in the ship's dining hall for up to 100 visitors, where the gospel and testimonies were shared. I tried to tailor my preaching to the local culture and situation. For example, when we docked in Colombo, Sri Lanka, I preached about the existence of God and his creation, explaining how Buddhists can be reconciled to God, even though they do not believe in creation and think sin is only dealt with through successive reincarnations. Consequently, our shipmates at first mistakenly thought this would be the main thrust of my ministry in other ports!

Many Buddhist monks visited the ship in their saffron robes. They tried to convince us that their religion was superior to Christianity, claiming, "You Christians kill people, but we are peaceful!" Not long after, Sri Lanka was plunged into civil war, with reports of gangs of Buddhists, including monks, killing Hindus in the streets. Christians also became victims of Buddhist persecution, with churches forcibly closed and destroyed and Christians maltreated and even murdered. So much for the Buddhists' claims of being a peaceful religion!

After Sri Lanka, we sailed to Calcutta (now Kolkata) in the Bay of Bengal. I was fascinated by this huge, chaotic city, home to a Bengali majority—a people who first heard the gospel two hundred years earlier through William Carey. For a month, we docked on the Hooghly River, a distributary of the Ganges. The Ganges is the holiest river for Hindus, and many desire to be cremated on its banks. However, due to financial struggles, it was common to see corpses floating past us down the river, as poor families found it difficult to purchase enough wood for cremation.

From India we crossed the Bay of Bengal to Malaysia and Singapore, where I became the latest in a long line of foreigners to offend the locals over their beloved durian fruit. When I visited a shop to buy some sweets for our children, I found a new brand of candy called durian toffee. I was curious and bought some. Jill and I both tasted one and quickly spat it out because it tasted rotten! A Chinese Malaysian lady came to our cabin and noticed the toffees languishing in our waste bin. When we explained that they were rotten, she strongly protested, "No, they are not!" and retrieved them to enjoy at her leisure. She then enlightened us about the true nature of the durian.

Durian trees grow in the forests of Southeast Asia and bear fruit a bit larger than a coconut. When the spiked fruit is opened, it reveals seeds surrounded by a messy pulp with a terrible smell. It is a treasured delicacy with a delicious taste for those who can ignore its stench. Alas, as an ignorant Westerner, I could never get past the putrid smell, which I would describe as a combination of pig excrement, turpentine, and onions, garnished with a sweaty gym sock!

While in Singapore, our seven-year-old son, Tim, spoke with a local man about the ship and invited him to visit. He came, and as far as we can tell, it was through this invitation that he came to know Jesus. Our month in Singapore was one of the highlights of our year on the *Logos*. We connected with many people there, some of whom became lifelong friends.

I was invited to speak in many churches around Singapore and received a warm welcome. It was the early days of a movement of Singaporeans serving as missionaries. By this time, we had copies of *Operation World* available, which were widely distributed at our meetings, enhancing the value of my preaching and the overall profile of the ship.

In Singapore, we held our very first Operation World Conference. We used a huge, empty warehouse in the port area to host the day-long event, which was attended by about 1,000 people. Operation World Conferences were subsequently hosted in every port and on every continent in the decades that followed. I believe these conferences played a significant role in disseminating the challenge of the Great Commission around the world and contributed to the size and composition of the global mission force today.

With each speaking engagement, I gradually built up my collection of visual aids. Overhead projectors were becoming more widely used in churches, so I began creating my own diagrams and maps. With only color transparency pens and a ruler available on the ship, my initial diagrams were very rudimentary. However, the number and variety of transparencies steadily increased as we traveled.

When we docked in Melbourne five months later, someone asked why we were using such poor overhead transparencies. This feedback deflated me after all the time and effort I had spent making them! I determined that once we were settled in England, I would learn how to create quality transparencies. The resulting improvement had a widespread and dramatic effect in the 1980s and beyond.

Our journey continued, with stops in East Malaysia, the Philippines, and Papua New Guinea, followed by visits to Australia, New Zealand, and the island nations of the South Pacific. In the fascinating country of Papua New Guinea—home to more than 850 distinct tribes and languages—our first port of call was the little town of Wewak on the northern coast, which has a population of 3,000. We spent two days in the port, and almost the entire population came on board to visit the book exhibition.

During Jill's nursing career in London, she had been used by the Lord to lead a patient to Jesus, resulting in the conversion of the entire family. The patient's husband, Don, was a typewriter mechanic. After several years, God called the family to serve with Wycliffe Bible Translators, and they went on to serve for many years in Papua New Guinea. Jill felt a strong desire to visit them, but the challenge was how to get to the Highlands where the Wycliffe base was located. When Jill naively asked the locals waiting to board if anyone was traveling by road to the Bible translation hub of Ukarumpa, she was quickly informed that no road existed between Wewak and Ukarumpa. The conversation was overheard by a missionary family, the Gibletts, who were standing nearby. The father said, "We are traveling there tomorrow by plane, and we have spare seats!" Jill looked at them and exclaimed, "I know you!" The Gibletts were members of a church in Essex where Jill had grown up. You can imagine the surprise!

It was quickly arranged for Jill and our three children to fly to Ukarumpa the following day while I remained behind for prearranged ministry on the ship. At the airfield, there were two missionary planes scheduled to take off around the same time—one carrying the Giblett and Johnstone families and the other a Mission Aviation Fellowship twin-engine plane headed to a different destination. Tragically, the MAF flight crashed that day, killing all ten people on board. Apparently, the mechanic servicing the plane had been interrupted while reassembling the carburetor, leaving the bolts untightened. During the flight, the nuts worked loose, causing fuel to leak. With thick jungle below and very few landing strips, the desperate pilot had no hope of landing safely. I joined the family later, traveling by road from Madang to the Highlands. The journey involved fording eighteen rivers and navigating steep mountains. There were only two roads connecting the coast to the highland mountain ranges of the interior, highlighting both the importance and danger of missionary aviation in such an environment.

We sailed south from Papua New Guinea along the Great Barrier Reef to the Australian city of Brisbane, and then on to Sydney and Melbourne. It was memorable for both Jill and me to meet our new WEC colleagues in each of these cities. In Sydney, we were moored almost directly under the huge Sydney Harbour Bridge and opposite the Opera House—two of Australia's most iconic structures.

After six weeks in Australia, we crossed the Tasman Sea to New Zealand, a voyage that took five days. We encountered what is known as the "Roaring Forties," where strong southerly winds blow almost continuously with little land to interrupt the eastward flow at that 40-degree latitude. Most crew members were seasick due to the unpleasant motion of the ship. We kept little food down and arrived in New Zealand exhausted from the journey, only to be thrust into a flurry of activities awaiting us in Wellington and then Auckland.

Over the years, many people have asked what my favorite country is. Without a doubt, it is New Zealand, for its atmosphere, culture, scenery, and cleanliness. The main downside is its isolation and distance from almost everywhere else in the world!

Our final month was spent visiting the small Pacific nations of Tonga, Samoa, and Fiji, where we experienced the extraordinary hospitality and kindness of those beautiful people. In Fiji, we left the ship and began a series of flights. We eventually touched down in London several days later, where we received a warm welcome from our families just before Christmas 1979.

The year we spent traversing the world's oceans was a tremendous time for our family and ministry. One significant benefit was the widespread use of *Operation World*. At most ports, I received letters and new information, which allowed me to steadily update the text on my portable typewriter. During our first three months in England, I prepared all my material for a revised edition of the book requested by the publisher, which was published in 1980. What should have been a gentle introduction to a totally different ministry instead became a frantic rush.

The critical feedback I received in Melbourne about my overhead transparencies led to the development of an extraordinary array of resources. By 1982, we had distributed eight hundred sets of new transparencies to mission organizations, fulfilling a need among many churches and ministries. This effort created a small industry at the WEC headquarters dedicated to producing them.

Initially, I used colored translucent or hatched acetate sheeting, trimmed with a sharp blade, and applied press-on lettering. Each map or diagram took some hours to create. Several years later, we purchased a Kodak color photocopier, which we put to good use making stunning reproductions of the original diagrams and maps that I was designing. These reproductions proved so popular that, over the life of that machine, we sold over £110,000 worth of transparencies, helping to fund our office costs for many years.

On a personal level, the experiences we shared during our year at sea have lasted a lifetime. Peter, who turned ten on the ship, loved spending time on the bridge and in the wheelhouse, where he learned to update sea charts and act as helmsman. He was even awarded a helmsman's certificate. He later won school and university scholarships with the Royal Air Force, which funded his engineering degree before he embarked on a long and successful career as a math teacher.

Tim, our second son, loved life on the ship so much that after school he joined OM and served on the sister ship, the *MV Doulos*, for three years as a seaman-evangelist. One of the skills he learned was firefighting. He later became a fireman in the United Kingdom.

Ruth was only six when we arrived on the ship. Once, while sailing in the Bay of Bengal, huge waves caused the vessel to gyrate in a jerky corkscrew motion. A particularly vigorous wave caused Ruth to lose her footing, and she rolled under the lifeboat toward the raging sea, where there was no protective railing. At the last moment, she managed to grab hold of something that stopped her from falling overboard, just as the captain stripped off his coat, expecting to dive off the bridge to save her. In later life, Ruth and her husband, Andy, went to Turkey as church-planting missionaries, and they now serve as vicar and wife of a parish near Manchester.

The *MV Logos*, meanwhile, continued to spread the good news of God's salvation around the world until it tragically ran aground and sank off the tip of South America in January 1988. Fittingly, the site where it was finally laid to rest is known as "World's End." The rough waters of the Cape Horn area did not overcome the vessel until it had hosted approximately 10,000 crew members from around the world and impacted the lives of millions of people in more than 150 countries and territories. In the years following the demise of the original *MV Logos*, Operation Mobilization replaced it with *Logos II*, and today, the *Logos Hope* continues the legacy of mission ships that are changing the world for Christ.

16

Burnout

After five incredibly full and challenging years of ministry in Africa, raising three children, and a 12-month stint crossing the world's oceans—all while completing a new edition of *Operation World*—Jill and I needed a good rest and time to recover.

Our time on the *Logos* had been both rewarding and the most exhausting of my life. I ended up leading two or three conferences per day when we were in port, alongside daily pastoral ministry to the crew members.

At the end of our sea voyage, we should have had six months off for rest and recuperation before fully transitioning to WEC. However, they had graciously permitted us to delay our arrival, and I didn't want to disappoint them any further. Without any break, we immediately began the challenge of adjusting to a completely new mission culture as we transitioned from the Dorothea Mission to the leadership team of a large global Christian mission. The internal pressure that drove me stemmed from a sense of loyalty, first to the Lord and my family, but also to the organizations I was part of. We had committed to being part of the WEC team but had asked for a postponement to accommodate our year aboard the *MV Logos*, which WEC graciously granted. I felt indebted to them, so I didn't turn away any opportunity to serve for the next few years.

After the third edition of *Operation World* was published by Send the Light in 1978, George Verwer's global advertising led to a considerable response from readers, including valuable corrections and updated information. I also expanded my network of friends, who provided input and proofreading of information about the countries they knew well. In turn, they became ardent advocates for *Operation World*. My publishers needed to do a new print run, so were under pressure to provide a new edition as soon as possible.

I completed the revision by April 1980, but not without personal sacrifice. We should have been resting and settling into our new mission, but the pressure of meeting the publishing deadline made that impossible. Those first three months of transition were a hectic rush to finalize the manuscript. In the pre-internet age, obtaining information required writing to people in other countries, visiting specialist libraries, or clipping and filing magazine articles, which we stored in our multiple filing cabinets. During our long absence from the United Kingdom, Jill and I had grown blissfully unaware of how dramatically both British society and church culture had changed. Occasional visits home to preach did not reveal what life was really like. I learned firsthand that there is a world of difference between visiting a place and living there.

Although we were back in our homeland, it no longer felt the same. We had to relearn how to function in Britain, and we even needed to retake our driving tests to restore our UK licenses. Only in recent years have mission agencies begun to address the challenges of not only the culture shock experienced by workers they send overseas but also the confusion of "reverse culture shock" when missionaries return home after their time abroad.

In many ways, reverse culture shock is more complex than what most people experience when they first go to the mission field. When a person moves to another culture, they expect stress and challenges to overcome, so they prepare for it. However, many return to their homelands years later expecting to fit right back in, but it rarely happens that easily. During their absence, the culture, their church, and their circle of friends have all changed. More importantly, those serving in other countries have been changed by their experiences and are no longer able to fit in. They feel like strangers in their own homeland, which can have devastating effects.

For our children, life and school in Rhodesia were their normal; Africa was the continent of their birth and their home. They had been exposed to a rich variety of experiences that were unrelated to what they found in England. To them, England felt alien, and they struggled to adjust.

Our eldest child, Peter, found it the hardest to adapt, as the peer pressure from his classmates was more intense than what his younger siblings faced. At the age of ten, Peter was already a world traveler, and was accustomed to living among many cultures and languages. He had even learned to read and correct Admiralty nautical charts and was qualified to steer a large ship!

When we first returned to England, we couldn't understand why Peter was so eager to watch worldly music shows on television. We soon discovered that it wasn't the music he liked; he desperately needed a common topic of conversation with his classmates. They recognized that Peter was different and that he was wise about the world while being strangely ignorant of local customs, so they nicknamed him "The Religious Professor."

Peter processed this well, telling us, "I realized I was being persecuted for being different, so I thought I might as well be persecuted for being a Christian." On Sundays, he preferred to listen to the excellent teaching in the main adult church service rather than join the youth program. His reasoning was interesting: "I don't mind being persecuted as a Christian at school, but I do object to it at church!"

The original headquarters of WEC were in the London home of the mission's renowned founder, C. T. Studd. In 1969, WEC purchased the semi-derelict Bulstrode House and Park, which comprised over seventy acres of gardens, farmland, and woods. Although ownership of Bulstrode changed frequently over the centuries, its long and fascinating history can be traced back to the legendary Knights Templar, who owned the property in 1308 until they were suppressed by the King of England in 1337. Now,

Bulstrode became a beloved home for our family, along with all the challenges of living with over one hundred people in the same sprawling building.

For the next three decades, I was greatly blessed to serve as part of WEC's leadership team. It had never happened before that someone from a non-WEC background was given a top leadership role, and I would not easily advocate for such a step again. I think the measure of success we experienced was largely due to the graciousness and godliness of my co-leaders rather than to anything we did ourselves. I cannot remember a single occasion when we had a serious breakdown in relationships during all those years and with successive leaders.

It is curious that I, an outsider, appear to be the only person alive who sat under the ministry of every WEC International director except C. T. Studd, who died in 1931. He was succeeded by Norman Grubb, who became a very special friend to us in his final years. In the 1960s, Norman's writings had deeply impacted me while I was in Africa, but I never dreamed he would one day become our close friend as he progressed into his 90s.

When Jill and I came to WEC, it was well understood that we would continue our ministry commitments to keep producing *Operation World*. In the ensuing years, my two parallel ministry worlds blended into a symbiotic oneness that I believe enhanced both. My colleagues were always generous in allowing me the time to complete the extensive work of preparing new editions of the book.

God had brought us back to England for a purpose much larger than we ever anticipated. We saw numerous answers to prayer, supernatural deliverances, and amazing advancements of the gospel around the world, all while living and serving in the supportive environment of the WEC headquarters in Bulstrode. Leslie and Jill Brierley left behind a godly heritage for us to emulate. They also passed their Bulstrode office to us, along with filing cabinets filled with information and some rather archaic furniture. The office itself overlooked an inner courtyard surrounded by a two-story brick extension of the main building.

As part of a community of around one hundred people, we were all required to perform menial tasks to keep the headquarters functioning. We took turns driving children to school, cooking, and doing housework. Visitors to Bulstrode were astonished to find us with aprons on, washing dishes and cleaning up after meals. We wanted to model servant leadership, so although these duties were challenging to maintain with our constant travel and exhaustion, we willingly embraced them.

As I began this new ministry, one of my initial goals was to gain a thorough understanding of WEC and the different fields around the world, as well as to get to know as many of my fellow workers as possible. Over the next four years, I came to personally know seven hundred to eight hundred of our one thousand one hundred workers serving in over thirty countries.

One of the spin-offs of my leadership and authorship was an increased association with international movements focused on world evangelization. Chief among these were my involvement with the Lausanne Movement in the 1980s and later the AD2000 and Beyond Movement, led by Luis Bush in the 1990s. I became a spokesperson for pioneering missions like WEC within these movements.

I was invited to join the Lausanne Committee's Strategy Working Group, chaired by Ed Dayton of World Vision. This opportunity allowed me to give input into the intense discussions among Christians at that time as they struggled to define terms such as "hidden peoples," "evangelization," and "people groups." Much of the terminology now taken for granted in the missions world originated during that period.

I was a first-time contracted author and a novice in negotiating with publishers. The leaders of Send the Light had missionary hearts and passion for prayer, but they were also running a publishing business led by one of the most generous and unorthodox book distributors of the twentieth century—George Verwer. For the 1978 edition, Send the Light had offered me royalties of just 2 percent of net sales, on the basis that this book was a financial risk. As a novice, I didn't realize this was a publisher's starting negotiating position and not necessarily a final offer, so I meekly accepted their terms. However, for the 1980 edition, we managed to negotiate an increased royalty rate of 5 percent of net sales. In other words, the royalties are calculated based on wholesale bulk sales, which are often priced 20–50% below the recommended retail price.

Occasionally, I hear of people who assume that I must be rich from all the book sales. If only they knew the truth! The income I received from the books was far less than many people assumed, and all the earnings were reinvested into our office expenses or allocated toward the cost of producing the next edition. The fact is, the income didn't even come close to covering our costs.

Looking back, I realize that the early 1980s was a *kairos* moment in missions, though it was not easy to discern at the time. The global awakening that began in the early 1960s was gaining momentum, with large numbers of young people in Western nations converting and multitudes turning to God in Africa, Latin America, and parts of Asia. Many youth movements wanted to spread the gospel but had little accessible information about the world. Numerous small mission movements were launched in countries that had never previously realized they had a responsibility to help fulfill the Great Commission.

The 1980 edition of *Operation World* resulted in several significant outcomes, notably a considerable increase in demands on our time. We needed a team to manage the burgeoning responsibilities, but at that time, our research office consisted of just me and my secretary! For the next several years, I traveled to every continent (except Antarctica), speaking at conferences, global gatherings, churches, and student groups. I invariably tried to combine my trips with ministry at WEC bases around the world, visiting key countries such as the United States, Indonesia, Brazil, and Nigeria.

As an example of how the Lord of the Harvest was orchestrating events for his glory, in 1980 I spoke at an Operation World Conference in Brazil, where a young Brazilian woman, Najua Dibo, asked me how she could go to Albania to preach the gospel. At that time, the Albanian Communist regime boasted that they had eliminated all religious influence from their nation, claiming to be the first fully atheist country in the world. I told her that Albania seemed to be off-limits, but if she could find her way to Kosovo in nearby Yugoslavia, she would find many Albanians there and could learn their language and culture.

Najua went to Kosovo, and when Communism collapsed in 1992, she was one of the first missionaries to enter the country, planting a church in the capital, Tirana. She had an amazing God-given influence on the country for the next three decades, and when she died in 2020, Albanian television broadcast a 15-minute special program on her life, interviewing many people who had been impacted by her message.

Almost a decade later, Jill and I were invited by our West African WEC teams to The Gambia, Senegal, and Guinea-Bissau. During our travels, we met two Brazilian New Tribes Mission workers who were waiting on the tarmac for their plane to take them back to their ministry base. One of the Brazilians ran up to me and gave me a warm embrace. He explained, "I came to Senegal because you spoke at an Operation World Conference in 1980. Thank you!" The other Brazilian added, "Are you the one who wrote that book on the world? That is also why I am here!"

Throughout history, many servants of Jesus have been caught up in the excitement of participating in his kingdom. However, even the strongest and most courageous Christian still faces the reality of living in a frail human body. I was, in effect, trying to do three full-time tasks in authoring books, strategizing for my mission, and public ministry to the wider church. As the Apostle Paul wrote to the believers in Corinth, we "have this treasure in jars of clay" (2 Cor 4:7), and "though outwardly we are wasting away, yet inwardly we are being renewed day by day" (2 Cor 4:16). All believers need balance and godly wisdom to live and serve in a healthy manner. God declares that we are "fearfully and wonderfully made" (Ps 139:14). We are not robots; even in the midst of a powerful revival, our bodies and minds still need rest and exercise, and we must nourish our bodies with a healthy diet. If we neglect these needs, it will only be a matter of time before we collapse.

By 1982, I generally felt happy and fulfilled, with a wonderful family and ministry environment. But I had been burning the candle at both ends for too long, and I suffered a severe life-changing burnout after not being able to sleep at all for weeks leading up to my collapse. During the previous three years, I would fall asleep whenever I sat down to rest, but eventually, I stopped being able to sleep at all. This led to a rapid decline as deep exhaustion overwhelmed me. I had tried to do too much for too long, and it was as if my body went on strike and cried out, "You ignored my warnings about needing sleep, so now you will have to live without it!" I had to stop everything—all appointments and preaching commitments were canceled until further notice.

By God's grace and with the loving support of my family and colleagues, I gradually recovered, but it took many years before I fully understood what had driven me to that point. My main issue was an excessive sense of loyalty to organizations and co-workers. Only after accepting that I was over-loyal and too eager to please others was I able to begin addressing the problem. I had to learn to say "no" to people and to take time to slow down and recognize my limitations.

My burnout fundamentally changed my life in many ways, and even today—more than forty years later—my sleep patterns have never fully recovered. I still struggle to get more than five hours of sleep each night. Whenever I see someone on a pathway similar to the one I was on, I plead with them to take urgent action. It's much better to rest for three months and pull back from the edge of a cliff than to face decades of lasting damage.

17

A Research Team

In the aftermath of my 1982 breakdown, I prayerfully reassessed my life and ministry with the help of Jill and some close friends. One conclusion we reached was that I was carrying a far too heavy workload for one man, and I needed a stronger support team to share the load.

Jill joined me as the full-time manager of our research office. She was invaluable, becoming the focal point for a team that could now expand. Jill coordinated with the WEC headquarters and organized the growing amount of information that flowed into the research office each week. She held everything together during the times I traveled overseas.

Jill took on the role of processing information received through letters and in mission publications. This was no small task, as thousands of letters and hundreds of journals and magazines continually poured in. She organized the incoming information into our filing cabinets and placed key articles into plastic binders for each country, further divided by subject, in our reference library. This was a huge help to me as I researched and compiled text for each country, and it became a valuable resource for hundreds of missionary candidates and others seeking information on prospective fields of service. Working with a research team was a very different experience for me. Much of my office time was spent managing WEC responsibilities, so a large proportion of my writing was done before breakfast and in the evenings. Jill carried much of the responsibility for building team dynamics and creating opportunities that suited each person's gifts from the stream of people God raised up to give us the help we needed—WECers and volunteers who came to assist for shorter or longer terms.

Jill was a loving and caring leader, with a special heart for missionaries who were recovering from sickness or burnout. At that time, the prevailing attitude was that if a worker had a problem, they simply needed to seek the Lord and resolve it on their own. Our research office became a safe haven for wounded workers to recover, and many were restored to ministry under Jill's loving supervision.

As Jill developed this aspect of her ministry, God reawakened in her a long-held vision to write a children's equivalent of *Operation World*. At just the right time, God provided teams of volunteers for each edition of *Operation World* and for the office's overwhelming flow of information and requests for help. Our volunteers ranged from those who worked a few hours a week to others who stayed with us for years.

As a visual learner, I wanted my readers and listeners to better understand my presentations through maps, photos, and diagrams. I hoped this would give them a better sense of God's glorious work in the world and the crushing needs in a lost world yet to be evangelized. To streamline our information, we purchased cameras and duplicators and photographed the thousands of collected pages onto microfiche, so that people could access them from anywhere in the world. With the microfiche system, we could send seventy-two pages of information in an ordinary letter. We marveled at these technological advancements, never dreaming how much easier things would become with the invention of the internet, which was still a decade away.

My public ministry was a key component in giving me real-life contact with the very people we wanted to influence and involve in world evangelization. It kept me grounded, even if it often meant being up in the air. During a visit to California in 1983, I used some of our maps in my presentation. Bob Waymire, a former rocket engineer, was enthusiastic about the maps and said they must be computerized. The idea sparked the founding of a new ministry called the Global Mapping Project, which later moved to Colorado Springs and became Global Mapping International (GMI). A strong partnership between GMI and the *Operation World* team emerged over the following decades.

GMI was joined by some remarkably talented people who revolutionized the way mission to unreached peoples was presented. Pete Holzmann developed the brilliant Atlas mapping software, while Loren Muehlius, a computer cartographer, undertook the extraordinary task of using details from the *Ethnologue* to digitally map the locations of all the languages in the world. This had never been done before.

I look back in awe at how the Lord connected me with so many brilliant men and women, creating a synergy that enhanced the global advance of the gospel during the 1980s and 1990s.

The first three editions of *Operation World* were compiled without computers or a database. All my statistics were painstakingly written on paper and added up with a calculator; statistical calculations were derived using a slide rule and graph paper. It is hard to imagine such a process in today's world. Indeed, I am acutely aware that many readers may not even understand the concept or some of the terms I have just used.

In 1978, I visited Kenya for a month to work with David Barrett on his *World Christian Encyclopedia*. He had recently been given funds to purchase a computer, and I had the privilege of working on a Taiwan-made Wang machine, which boasted a massive detachable disk drive and used 8-inch floppy disks for data transfer. I marveled at what David's programmer could achieve with just a few lines of code, as both storage space and memory were at a premium.

The disk drive proved vital when David was expelled from Kenya because some corrupt individuals were angry that he would not use his computer to print banknotes for them. It was the first computer I had ever worked on, and was probably the only one in all of Kenya at that time. Although I couldn't fully grasp how pivotal computers would become to my work and to society overall, that initial exposure made me realize we needed to transition to computers sooner rather than later.

While attending a conference in Thailand, Ed Dayton from World Vision offered us financial support to purchase a computer for the next edition of *Operation World*. Thanks to this generous gift, we aimed high and bought a multi-user system with an impressive hard-drive storage capacity of 40 MB. Today, my cell phone has memory more than two hundred times larger. However, we had one problem: it was the first computer in WEC, and nobody had a clue how to make it work for us.

The Lord Jesus always has impeccable timing. An Australian computer expert, Ian Case, and his wife Chris had just completed their two-year training course at the WEC base in Tasmania. Ian was wondering how to use his skills in mission work, and they soon joined us at Bulstrode. We ran six terminals from this one computer—two of which we made available to our international office about 100 yards away in the main building. The system worked well for several years—until we had a thunderstorm. We had not anticipated the impact lightning would have on our wiring and were forced to make expensive repairs to restore our computer and terminals.

When our system was functioning properly, it revolutionized our office work and transformed how we handled correspondence. Email had not yet been developed, so all our correspondence was still conducted by postal mail leading up to the publication of the 1986 edition of *Operation World*. Nonetheless, our computer sped up the whole process by giving us easily editable and reproducible letters and files.

With Ian Case's prompting and help, we began the massive task of transferring our global statistics into electronic spreadsheets and an early database program. The most important files contained data on the world's religions and Christian denominations. We had entered the computer age, and great advances in our work soon followed due to the new technology.

18

A MEGA-SHIFT AT WEC

We stepped into our leadership role at WEC during a crucial time, which we only began to appreciate a decade later. Reflecting on WEC's history, I realized that crucial times of re-envisioning seemed to come in 16-year intervals. C. T. Studd had been used by God to launch WEC as a pioneering mission in 1913. Sixteen years later in 1929, his son-in-law Norman Grubb took charge, and under his leadership, WEC received a fresh vision from the Lord. The overall pioneering culture was retained, but the way the mission operated was transformed and refreshed.

Norman emphasized prayer as a fundamental aspect of our culture. Seeking God's guidance for the future direction of the work was done collectively as a fellowship of workers. New teams were established worldwide to operate based on these principles. Decisions were made by workers in the field who elected their own leaders, rather than directives being issued from the mission headquarters in England.

Under God's hand, the range of WEC's work expanded, spreading from Africa to Asia, the Middle East, and South America. Hundreds of unevangelized people groups heard the Good news for the first time, and tens of thousands became disciples of Jesus. Leslie Brierley was asked to conduct global surveys to identify where WEC should focus for its next advance.

His findings were released in 1945 and again in 1961—sixteen years apart. Each initiative led to a large increase in the number of fields and new recruits.

According to this cycle, the next re-envisioning should have occurred in 1977, but the opportunity was missed. The mission began to lose momentum, with the number of home staff increasing while the number of workers on the field declined. When we arrived in 1980, we found a rather discouraged mission organization. Some argued that WEC had expanded too quickly and should consolidate. I countered by arguing that we should never recruit new workers just to maintain existing ministries; rather, we needed fresh vision to advance and claim new territories for Christ. In the process, others would also be recruited who would be better suited for older fields. Being part of a visionary pioneer organization is far more attractive for most people, even for those better fitted for sustaining and supportive ministries.

In 1978 we committed to holding international leaders' conferences (InterCon) every six years, with the next one scheduled for 1984. Our International Office team and a few core leaders gathered in 1982 for a planning meeting at our German headquarters in Epstein, Germany. The two major issues we had to address were our future international leaders and the program content and emphases for the 1984 InterCon. I was expected to lay the framework for our next, overdue visionary advance and was given two full days to present my case, so I went conscious a significant weight rested on my shoulders. I had several supportive positives: I had done much research on both countries and peoples, and *Operation World*, along with a recently completed slideshow based on our work on maps and transparencies, had proven successful and was being widely used around the world. I also asked that we *not* publish a long list of goals for new fields, unevangelized peoples, and ministries beforehand; instead, we should prepare well for fields and regions to agree together what those goals should be.

In 1978, it was agreed that all fields and ministries would be grouped into geographical regions, each advised by a regional leader couple. The basic commitment to fields being self-governing meant that this structural change was not universally well received as it was perceived as a threat to that level of autonomy. Therefore, I proposed that we restructure the three weeks assigned to this InterCon, and give the middle week *solely* to regions meeting together, so that all the visions and goals generated could coalesce into a mission-wide envisioning for the future. This proposal was agreed upon and it worked amazingly well when implemented two years later.

We also addressed the leadership question. Robert and Isobel Mackey had served faithfully as our leaders, but Robert's health was failing, and he wanted to hand over his role. He came with a strong suggestion that stunned us all: he believed that God had shown him a WEC couple serving in Indonesia, Dieter and Renate Kuhl. After this initial revelation, he asked Isobel to pray for guidance without revealing his thoughts. Amazingly, after prayer, she also identified the Kuhls! What confirmation! Most of us gathered there hardly knew them, but they had become close friends after Dieter led me on a three-month ministry tour of Indonesian fields in 1981. I was delighted.

The complication was that they were leading a key missionary seminary in Indonesia and could not be released for three years. We had to find an interim leader, and it took a whole day of agonizing discussion before we asked Stewart and Marie Dinnen from Australia to serve as International Directors. These recommendations were presented to the entire WEC team, which approved this leadership. Stewart was a dynamic, fast-acting leader who proved to be just the right leader to enourage fields and ministries to follow through on their commitments. Dieter followed in 1986 and became a wise, strategic leader who solidified the massive advances made in the two decades after 1984.

In June 1984, we gathered for our big InterCon at Kilkreggan on the Clyde in Scotland. God met with us and set a new course for WEC in terms of visions, new ways of working, and structures that could sustain them. I was the first main speaker and had two full days for presenting and discussing the new advances. I began by giving a global overview of the progress in world evangelization, highlighting what God was doing before addressing the challenges.

At that time, Communism was still the great threat, and the Cold War was at its height. China was emerging from the dark years of Maoist oppression, with reports indicating that the church there had not only survived the terrible persecution of the Cultural Revolution but had also grown exponentially in many places. The world of Islam, however, showed few signs of breakthrough for the gospel, except in Indonesia. I advocated that, as a pioneering church-planting mission, we needed to refocus on our God-given mandate to go where others had not yet gone. I dedicated much of my time to presenting the challenges faced by the Turkic, Kurdish, Arab, Tibetan, and Malay peoples.

The middle week of the conference yielded positive results, and the regional leaders bonded effectively for the first time. We then collated all the contributions, and at the end of the conference, we summarized our findings. I mention several conclusions here because of their significance for us as a mission and their impact on new patterns of mission involvement that influenced my own ministry in writing, strategizing, and speaking.

- Every field and ministry set goals, and from this emerged some regional goals as well.
- I estimated that we needed eight hundred new workers to achieve these goals—an almost doubling of our workforce. Thus we adopted the mission-wide slogan "800 for the '80s." I believe we nearly achieved this.
- We moved from a country approach to a people approach, opening the door to trans-national fields, and out of this emerged new fields for the Kurds and Central Asian Muslim peoples, that aimed to reach the people groups within such clusters.
- We changed our name from Worldwide Evangelization Crusade, as the "crusade" part was not helpful for our increasing efforts to reach the Muslim world. We became

Worldwide Evangelization for Christ, and by 1990, we had become the international agency with the largest number of missionaries focused on the Muslim world.
- We truly became an international mission. I proposed that we prepare for an influx of new missionaries from other parts of the world. At that time, there were only about a dozen non-Caucasian WEC workers from anywhere in the world. I advocated for readiness to welcome Koreans, Brazilians, Indonesians, Chinese, Nigerians, Indians, and others into WEC. We were unprepared for the enormous multicultural transformation that was coming, nor did we comprehend the impact this would have on how we operated and planted churches. But ready or not, God's kingdom was advancing in amazing ways throughout the world, and if WEC wanted to remain relevant, we had to embrace the mega-shift!

Under the Dinnens and Kuhls' dynamic leadership, the call to recruit new workers for the harvest field spread far and wide. Over the next decade, our number of workers increased from 1,100 in 1983 to nearly 2,000 by the end of the 1990s. We also doubled the number of our fields, many of which had to be kept confidential because they were located in countries with restricted access. Today, there are still about 2,000 workers involved with WEC, but our composition has changed dramatically. About half of our members are non-Westerners, with Koreans making up the largest ethnic component of our ministry.

I drew a set of four basic conclusions from my experiences with WEC's mega-shift, which I have sought to apply in every leadership role I have subsequently filled. They are: imposed visions do not work; those who implement the vision must be part of the decision-making process; the vision must be embraced by the whole organization; and the provision of resources will follow God's work.

We ended the conference with a remarkable prayer meeting as we committed ourselves to the God-given vision, realizing that this could entail hardships and suffering. I look back and see how privileged I am to have been part of the WEC leadership team in one capacity or another for thirty-two years. Over the years, we faced countless crises, including wars, field evacuations and closures, hostage situations, martyrdoms, medical emergencies, and moral failures. Although there have been times when we disagreed on the best way forward, I cannot recall a single occasion when the leadership team of WEC experienced a relational breakdown.

In most English translations of the Bible, Matthew 20:19–20 is rendered as, "Go and make disciples of all nations, baptizing them in the name of the Father and of the Son and of the Holy Spirit, and teaching them to obey everything I have commanded you." Here we have a translation problem. In the original Greek, the only active verb in the sentence is "disciple." The other verbs—"go," "baptize," and "teach"—are in the infinitive form: going, baptizing, teaching. The Greek uses "disciple" as both a noun and a verb, but many modern translations only recognize it as a noun. My preferred translation would be: "In going, disciple all nations . . ." This highlights that the ministry of discipleship is central to all our going. Consequently, whether you are a Bible translator, mission leader, teacher, pastor, administrator, professional, or secular worker, you are called to be a discipler as you seek to influence others to walk with Jesus and grow into ministry and leadership.

This realization helped me adjust my ministry perspective. When God called me to go as an evangelist to the slums of Africa, I understood that my primary calling was not just to win precious souls, but to disciple them as well. I gradually gained a clear understanding that discipling is my primary ministry, regardless of my job title.

After joining WEC, I was eager to integrate this discipling emphasis into my new leadership role. I also felt a mandate from

God to serve and disciple other mission agencies. *Operation World* played an important role in providing these new missions with the needed information to move forward. My special burden was for the many indigenous missions emerging in regions that Western churches still viewed as their target mission fields. Throughout the 1980s, there was a massive surge of interest among Asian, Latin American, and African churches to send their own missionaries to unreached peoples. At WEC, we wanted to contribute to these movements, and over time, we adopted what some may consider a radical approach. Instead of just wanting to plant churches or support work in unreached nations, we sought to establish entire mission agencies in those areas. They would be tools in God's hands, with the potential to impact whole countries with the gospel. Essentially, WEC was discipling new mission groups, helping them grow and become effective disciplers of others.

We began to see this vision unfold first in Brazil, Indonesia, and West Africa. We formed agreements with certain indigenous mission agencies we shared a common vision with, cooperating with them on every level. This resulted in WEC workers coming alongside them in the field, while some of their key workers came to Bulstrode for a form of internship, where they developed their gifts before returning home as better-equipped leaders.

Permeating every aspect of this plan was a bedrock commitment that we would not act in a paternal, controlling manner, lording it over our brothers and sisters. Instead of positioning ourselves in front or behind them, we aimed to walk alongside them, doing everything we could to help them become the people God called them to be and to effectively disciple the nations within their influence.

Numerous examples illustrate how this vision played out over the years, and I would like to share about one of our earliest partnerships. We formed an agreement with a young Nigerian ministry called CAPRO, or Calvary Ministries, which began in 1976 from a revival among Nigerian students. Our partnership flourished into a great mutual blessing, and CAPRO grew into an international mission with over seven hundred workers across the Muslim world. They have seen much fruit, planting churches in places where no gospel witness had previously existed.

Over many years, learning from numerous victories and failures, the concept of discipling as we evangelize the nations has become a reality. Whole mission agencies have been discipled in various lands, and the synergy created by our mutual cooperation has infused spiritual life into WEC. In effect, our indigenous brothers and sisters have discipled us as well.

(19)

1986— OPERATION WORLD 4

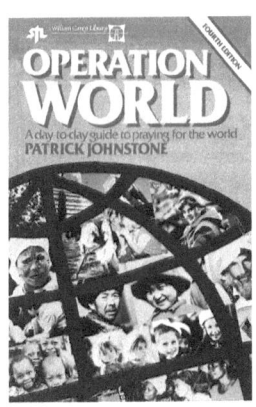

The largely successful implementation of our new strategy at WEC allowed me to focus on completing a new edition of *Operation World*. The third edition from 1980 was in serious need of revision due to the ever-changing world and the volume of new information. As my authoring momentum gathered pace, I dedicated every spare moment to researching and writing country profiles during the latter half of 1984 and much of 1985.

Initially, I wanted to bring out a new *Operation World* book every five years. However, this proved unrealistic and would have required a total commitment to my book-writing ministry alone. So I adjusted my plan and aimed to release a new edition after each of our major WEC International Leaders' Conferences, which occurred every six years. But I missed my targets slightly, and in the end, they were published in 1986, 1993, and 2001.

I introduced several improvements and innovations in the fourth edition, including an alphabetical listing of countries. Previous editions organized the book by world regions and then by country within each region, but this confused many people who were unsure what region a country belonged to. Calendar dates were assigned to each country, allowing readers to pray through the entire world in a year. While many countries were assigned a specific date, India and China were allocated an entire week each due to their size and complexity. Separate sections for the states of India and the provinces of China were introduced, as many of these regions are much larger in area and population than most countries.

Looking back, I am astonished at how we accomplished what we did before much of today's technology had even been imagined. God was good to us and led the whole process from start to finish. He always sent ideal people at just the right time, even though all work was voluntary and no team member received any pay. As we prayed, the right people would come to us.

As anyone who has written a book under the pressure of a deadline can testify, the months leading up to publication were intense. But when the files were finally sent to the publisher, a deep sense of relief came over me. As a team, we had done everything we could, and now the results were in God's hands.

For the 1986 edition, we had carefully selected fonts and diagrams, ensuring they were the minimum sizes for easy reading. Then, just two weeks before the book went to print, we received an excited phone call from the publisher. They had found a new printing company that could print the book at a significantly reduced price, but only if we agreed to shrink the page size by 15 percent. After they assured me that it would make little to no difference, I reluctantly agreed. Consequently, the statistical sections were so small that elderly readers and those with less than average vision had a significant problem reading the book. In our attempt to save money, the effectiveness of the book was diminished. It was a decision I still regret.

Despite this mistake, I believe the 1986 edition had several positive outcomes. More than 250,000 English copies were printed in the first run, along with tens of thousands more in Spanish, Portuguese, German, Korean, and other languages. A new set of seventy prayer cards was also printed.

One of the main reasons for the existence of *Operation World* is to instigate strategic prayer for the church and the fallen world we live in. Little did we know that the world was about to experience drastic change before the next edition would appear. The Berlin Wall fell in 1989, and the Soviet Union quickly disintegrated at the start of the 1990s, resulting in the formation of sixteen new countries.

I am sure that the fervent prayers of many Christians led to the dismantling of that massive atheistic system without a world war. The collapse of world powers has often occurred rapidly throughout history. In this case, the speed of change is perhaps best illustrated by the experience of Soviet cosmonaut Sergei Krikalev, who spent five months at the Mir Space Station in 1991. During that time, his home city of Leningrad was renamed St. Petersburg, and the Soviet superpower crumbled to such an extent that he was unable to return to Earth for another six months. Krikalev became known as "the last Soviet citizen."

The 1986 edition of *Operation World* also had a deep impact on my other ministry roles. Balancing my research and writing with my leadership role in WEC and the demands of public ministry was always a challenge. Despite the popularity of the books, I wanted my role in WEC to remain my primary focus. *Operation World* existed to serve the work of the ministry, not the other way around.

Many new speaking invitations came in from around the globe, and countless new doors of opportunity opened. Saying "no" to people was not my strong point, so my travel schedule quickly filled. I always sought to combine my conferences with WEC ministry in each country we visited.

In June 1986, Jill and I were asked by WEC to take on the role of deputy international directors to Dieter and Renate Kuhl. To manage the increased workload, we recruited a team of support staff that worked well together for years. Once all the components were in place, I believe the years that followed were the most productive of all my service in WEC. Dieter and I had a broad knowledge of our deployed workers and their ministries. We were both forward-thinking, and our stimulating brainstorming sessions led to many new ventures, resulting in the successful deployment of new teams among the unreached peoples of the world, with a special emphasis on the Arab world, the Turkic peoples of Central Asia, the Kurds, and the Mongolians.

As always, Jill was a pillar of strength for me, providing continuity and stability in our lives. In addition to creating a wonderful home environment as our three children attended school, she was the glue that held our research office together. As time progressed, my travels took me to many lesser-known unreached areas of the world. Jill joined me on one notable trip to one of the most unreached regions in far western Africa. During our travels, we visited northern Senegal, where the Senegal River forms the boundary between that country and Mauritania as it flows through the Western Sahara. In this churchless land, virtually untouched by the gospel, we stayed in the home of a missionary. The extreme heat and dust, combined with the constant effort to get rid of the piles of wind-blown sand that invaded every part of the house, deepened my admiration for believers serving in such challenging places.

On another trip, I visited the neighboring countries of Burkina Faso, Ghana, and Côte d'Ivoire. It was an eye-opening journey. In each country, an indigenous network of churches had emerged that were sending teams to unreached people groups. When we convened our first African conference, many church leaders were shocked to discover that there were other churches like theirs across Africa. As an interdenominational mission, we had been good in planting congregations, but not so good in developing networks of churches that impacted whole nations. This revelation gave them a sense of belonging to a movement far bigger than their own local networks. It also gave me an opportunity to check the *Operation World* text for these and other countries in the region.

Returning home to the Bulstrode office after visiting exotic destinations was always a challenge, with bulging files of letters to answer and many brainstorming sessions with other WEC leaders awaiting me. Like a drumbeat that permeated all other activities, the challenge of maintaining progress toward the next *Operation World* was constantly with me. Somehow, the Lord Jesus enabled us to juggle these responsibilities, and as a result, the 1980s became what I consider the most fruitful decade of my ministry.

At this time, a new perspective on the remaining task of world evangelization emerged when I saw a map that grouped most of the remaining unreached peoples into eight or nine blocs. Over time, I developed a concept that categorized all 17,000 people groups into fifteen "affinity blocs" and two hundred sixty "people clusters." Ultimately, this perspective influenced many international ministries, leading to significant restructuring away from a narrow country-oriented focus to one of engaging with cultures and peoples in their global context rather than within specific political nations.

This approach became increasingly important in the twenty-first century as long-term missionary visas became more difficult to obtain, and the flow of refugees surged due to climate change, war, and persecution. It became easier for missionaries to openly say, "I work among Kurds," without risking their security by specifying which Middle Eastern country or country of refuge they served in.

The need for security and confidentiality in our work was underscored by an incident at a conference I attended with about eighty other mission leaders. During a coffee break, a man rushed into the room and swept up all the papers strewn over the chairperson's table before being intercepted as he tried to leave the auditorium with his haul. It turned out he was a Muslim sent to gather information about our plans. This incident reminded us that how we handle sensitive information could endanger ministries and lives.

20

THE DECADE OF HARVEST

You may be reading this book in a place where the church does not seem to be growing, which may bring you discouragement. But are you aware that just a few decades ago, the world experienced a huge surge in the number of Christians? As a mission researcher, I would describe the 1990s as the "decade of harvest." In numerous countries, the body of Christ saw unprecedented growth at levels not experienced before and which perhaps may not be seen again.

The 1990s was an extraordinary decade for the kingdom of God, although it was not readily apparent at the time. The end of the Second World War marked the beginning of a 75-year period of relative stability worldwide, despite the continuation of many localized conflicts and the ongoing Cold War tensions between the West and the Communist Bloc. This stability created an environment where a massive expansion of technology and machinery boosted global industrialization, creating new opportunities for the spread of the gospel.

In terms of world evangelization, the 1990s represented the pinnacle of the 200-year missions movement initiated by the Moravians and William Carey in the eighteenth century, although the Dutch Reformed Church had sent out the first Protestant missionaries more than a century earlier. Many new fields opened to the gospel, yielding an unprecedented harvest.

I estimate that during the 1990s, the number of evangelical Christians grew from 282 million to 426 million globally, or, as a percentage of the world population, from 5.4 percent to 7 percent. To have 144 million new Evangelicals added to the church in a single decade is incredible. I refer to the spectacular growth of Christianity around the world between the 1960s and the end of the twentieth century as "The Sixth Awakening." Much of this growth went unnoticed by Western Christians, as it primarily occurred in countries and regions not previously considered open to the gospel, while the church in the West generally experienced decline over that same period.

Often, people view the world through the lens of their own experiences, as if it revolves around them and their cultural norms. If we're not careful, we can be deceived into thinking that if God isn't moving in our local community, then he isn't moving anywhere else.

From the time I first met her, Jill was always passionate about ministry to children, which was how God first called her to Africa. When she finally joined the Dorothea Mission to serve in the South African townships, she invariably took responsibility for the children's ministry. Jill was convinced that, although the Bible is profound, there is no truth in Scripture that a child cannot understand. She wanted believing children to be discipled and expected them to pray, testify, and preach about Jesus Christ. Jill also wrote several evangelistic tracts for children, and during her years in the South African townships, she saw God transform many lives.

When Jill married me, she left her childrens' ministry in South Africa, and together we began our life in Rhodesia, where she embraced the ministry of raising our three children. I so admired her skills as a mother. Jill's philosophy of motherhood was to concentrate her energy on these precious children until they started school. Once a firm foundation was laid, she felt confident that their lives would be set on the right course, and she would be freed up for wider ministry.

After we returned to England, as our children became more independent, Jill was gradually able to give more time to her ministry. Although her time for writing was limited, her long-held dream of writing a children's book still burned in her heart.

In 1989, Jill started a prayer club for the many children at Bulstrode, with about ten attending regularly. Her aim was to share information about a country or people group and then pray for them. This gave Jill the inspiration to write about more countries and peoples, leading to a unique concept for an upcoming book. The pattern Jill developed was remarkable. She selected 26 countries and 26 people groups for inclusion—two chapters for each letter of the alphabet. For A, she chose Albania and the Azeri people; for Z she selected Zimbabwe and the Zulu people. The fifty-two chapters were designed to enable readers to pray for one country or people group each week of the year.

Although Jill was not an artist, she had always wanted to be one. She began the illustrations, which were later developed by others. Mary Filidis of YWAM drew beautiful illustrations of the peoples, and Tony Kenyon contributed all the other artwork.

As mentioned earlier, Jill was a poet who could turn any fact or story into a beautiful and memorable poem. She incorporated this talent into the book by including pithy two-liners. Each two-line rhyme conveyed several key facts about the country or people, making them easy for children to remember. Here are several examples:

> *A is for Albania where Christians were banned,*
> *But God has stepped in and is changing this land.*

> *N is for New Zealand whose mountains are steep;*
> *The land of the kiwi and millions of sheep.*

> *P is for Papua New Guinea with people diverse;*
> *Many still fear the sorcerer's curse.*

> *T is for Tibetans who have a god-king.*
> *The Chinese removed him and rule from Beijing.*

> *V is for Vagla, whose musical tongue*
> *Can be spoken on an African drum.*

The first chapter Jill covered was Albania. At that time, the Communist dictator of the country was proudly boasting that he had banished all religious superstition from the land. All mosques and churches had been destroyed or converted for secular purposes.

This captured the imagination of the children in Jill's group, so they began to pray for Albania. At the time, Communism in Europe was beginning to collapse with nations like Poland, Hungary, and Czechoslovakia undergoing change, but there was no evidence of this yet in Albania. Then, in 1991, change suddenly swept through, and the country opened almost overnight. When Jill shared this news with the children's club, one girl was so excited that she jumped up and down, exclaiming, "We have changed Albania. We have changed Albania!" This inspired Jill's book title, *You Can Change the World*, which was ultimately published in 1992.

Jill was so busy with other ministry demands that she needed help to carve out time for research and writing. With no one on our small team able to assist, we set aside a day to fast and pray for a suitable coworker with the giftings to support her. On the appointed day, we prayed through the morning, and in the early afternoon, the phone rang. Our receptionist put through a call from the United States, and a lady introduced herself as Robyn Erwin. She explained that she had been using *Operation World* in her church to stimulate prayer for the world, and this caused her to think how much she would like to be involved in such a ministry. She asked if we had a vacancy.

I was astonished and could barely contain my excitement at such a dramatic and quick answer to our prayers. I suggested she contact our local WEC representative, who happened to live in Robyn's home city of Sacramento, California. After hanging up, I shared the amazing news with Jill. We stopped praying and started to praise God for his miracle-working power! Within a few months, Robyn had completed the WEC candidate orientation and traveled to the United Kingdom to join our research office. Jill now had a coworker, allowing her to dedicate more time to her writing. Jill and Robyn became close friends, although my contact with Robyn was fleeting, as I worked from my own office in a nearby part of Bulstrode.

21

THE LORD CALLS JILL HOME

At the start of 1990, I had a special time of prayer with the Lord as I looked ahead to the challenges of the new decade. We were very busy and overstretched, but we also felt happy and fulfilled. While I was praying, the unmistakably clear voice of my Heavenly Father spoke to my heart in the stillness of the moment: "This year is going to bring great pain and loss. Be ready for it." It felt as if the sunny sky had suddenly been obscured by a dark cloud. I took careful note of this message but did not let it dominate my thoughts, nor did I share it with Jill. I began the new decade with a mixture of anticipation tempered by foreboding.

In the lead-up to our 1990 WEC leaders' conference, we were so busy that we decided to take a family holiday, which we spent relaxing at the rural property of my sister Caroline and her husband, Richard. They had a grass tennis court on the farmhouse lawn, so we played some tennis while we were there. Jill was not a keen tennis player, but she decided to give it a try. At one point, she swung her racket to hit the ball and cried out in pain, "Oh, my back!" After that, she suffered increasing pain in several vertebrae in her upper back. Initially, we attributed it to a back injury that we hoped would soon heal.

When we returned home, Jill went alone to see our doctor, but he brushed off her concerns and didn't even examine her back. We later learned that he had developed the impression that

Bulstrode was a large commune of cooped-up religious fanatics and believed that most of our ailments were due to the social pressures produced by living such insular lives. As a result, he just dismissed Jill's complaints of intense pain as a psychosomatic condition.

Some weeks later, with Jill still in pain, we booked another appointment to see our doctor, and this time I accompanied her. During the consultation, I listed several real problems that Jill was having and insisted that she be properly assessed. Our doctor took our concerns seriously this time, scheduling blood tests and an X-ray for a few days later. Jill went for her X-ray at our local hospital and was informed of a pathological break—indicating it was not an injury but rather was caused by some malady. The blood tests soon returned a diagnosis of cancer. I will never forget that dreadful drive back to Bulstrode with Jill as we grimly contemplated a drastically changed future.

Jill was hospitalized because of her disintegrated vertebra, which was followed by the collapse of another adjoining vertebra a month or two later. She was in hospital for several months before the specialists could definitively diagnose the cause of the break. Eventually, she was sent by ambulance to a specialist hospital in Oxford, where a spinal sample finally confirmed that she had secondary cancer. I asked if they could locate the primary cancer, but the oncologist informed us it would be almost impossible to find, as the area of the primary cancer could be so small that one could not locate them.

Jill began a series of visits to Oxford for radiotherapy. The treatment was successful in killing the cancer in her spine, but it was only a matter of time before the cancer spread to other parts of her body. Her shattered bones reconnected and fused to form a three-vertebra section in her spine, which allowed her some degree of movement and normalcy.

By this time, Peter, our eldest, was studying aeronautical engineering at Bristol University, while Tim was in Asian waters aboard Operation Mobilization's second ship, the *MV Doulos*. Ruth was the only one of our children still at home and was preparing to start university. In retrospect, we felt relieved that we had unexpectedly started a family so early in our married life. Now we faced the likelihood that Jill would soon depart this world to be with the Lord, but instead of our children being young and dependent on us, they were grown and leaving the family nest.

One memorable day, I knelt beside Jill as she lay in pain on our sofa. She burst into tears and cried out, "I will never see my grandchildren!" This was the saddest moment of our long bereavement process. We hugged each other and prayed for grace and strength. We had to rethink our future and how we would adjust as a family and in our various ministries. We decided that Jill should concentrate on finishing *You Can Change the World*, while Robyn would take responsibility for more of the office work. Jill made good use of her remaining time.

We soon discovered that many people find it difficult to relate to a cancer sufferer—especially when the diagnosis is terminal. We decided the best way to handle this was to quietly inform visitors of Jill's illness and then move on to other matters. Some Christians proved to be rather insensitive, making comments such as, "Have you done something wrong?" "Is there a curse on you?" "We know someone who is really gifted in praying for the sick," and "If you had a bit more faith, you would be healed!"

Jill wrote several articles about living with terminal cancer that were published. I was amazed at how many people contacted her to express how much they were blessed by her writing, especially those facing death or bereavement. I told Jill that in the remaining time we had together, I would set aside my work on *Operation World* and make caring for her my top priority. She firmly dismissed this idea, saying I had already made significant progress on the next edition, and if I delayed for a few years, I would need to start over again from scratch. I kept working on the book but canceled most of my travel during the eighteen months we had left together.

In June 1991, we went on a final holiday together. We hired a cabin cruiser on the Thames River and spent two weeks traveling the entire navigable length of the river, from London to Lechlade. It was a wonderful time, and Jill was at the healthiest part of her remission.

Toward the end of the year, we noticed that Jill was having increasing difficulty finding the right words in sentences. The cancer had spread to her brain and elsewhere. Radiotherapy was able to deal with the brain tumor, but she lost all her hair, and the steroids caused her face to puff up. Although she maintained her positive outlook and continued to crack jokes, we realized her time was short.

Jill involved our WEC colleagues Daphne Spraggett and Rosie Scott in the final stages of preparing for *You Can Change the World*. The text was completed just a week before she died.

In Jill's final days, blood clots appeared in her legs, causing her considerable pain as gangrene set in. She had difficulty sleeping during her final week but used her time to design a second volume of her book. She jotted down her ideas and asked Daphne to take on the project and see it through to publication. She also suggested that Daphne write her own volume and provided her with a notepad of ideas for her to explore.

Cancer is a much-feared disease, but terminal cancer has one positive aspect—it allows time to come to terms with bereavement. In our case, we had nearly two years. It was also a blessing that Jill retained a clear and alert mind. She maintained her loving, outgoing personality and her commitment to the Lord Jesus until the end.

Once, while I was praying, God spoke to my heart: "I have given you Jill for 23 years. Now it is my turn." This helped me release my beloved wife to him when the time was right. When the final crisis came, I felt a deep peace amid the agonizing sadness. Much of my grieving had been at its strongest a year earlier.

Jill died on June 17, 1992, just a few days before her 56th birthday. During her final two weeks, Jill's mother and her two sisters, June and Liz, were with us at Bulstrode. Tim was granted leave from the *MV Doulos*, which was then docked in the South Korean island of Cheju. He arrived home the evening before his mother died and was able to spend a brief time with her. Ruth and Peter were with us as well. What a comfort it was to have a loving and caring family at such a time.

Twenty-four years earlier, in October 1968, Glyn Davies had delivered the message at our wedding, based on Philippians 1:21: "For to me, to live is Christ and to die is gain." Glyn had emphasized the first part. Now, at the thanksgiving service for my beloved Jill, the same verse was shared with an emphasis on the second part. Although our hearts were heavy with grief, the children and I found comfort in knowing that Jill was now fully alive like never before. She was experiencing the "gain" of living and dying in Christ, and she was free from suffering forever!

I look back with admiration at all that Jill achieved during her last two years of suffering—not only in the lives she touched through her writing and counseling, but also posthumously through the publication of her books. For many years, people around the world have shared how much those books helped shape their worldview and introduced them to ministry in other cultures.

In 2016, twenty-four years after Jill's passing, I stayed with a Khasi Christian family in Shillong, a town in northeast India. The teenage daughter was so excited that she could hardly sleep the night before our arrival—she was going to meet the husband of the lady who wrote *You Can Change the World*! Her mother had read a chapter to her each night as a young child, which deeply shaped her life.

22

A Church for Every People by the Year 2000

As I walked through the grieving process after Jill's death in 1992, I remained the WEC director of research and the deputy to Dieter and Renate Kuhl, who led the ministry. It was during this time that the loss of Jill hit me hardest. She had become a vital conduit for so many relationships and a rock of stability in people's lives—something I could never be due to my constant travel. With Jill around, everything had flowed smoothly, but I struggled in her absence. I felt bewildered and realized I could no longer accomplish all I wanted or meet the expectations placed on me.

I also needed to fulfill my international obligations for both WEC and the AD2000 and Beyond Movement. Under the leadership of Luis Bush, the latter was in its early stages and needed help setting achievable goals, as well as providing the vision and tools to reach them. My long involvement with the AD2000 and Beyond Movement dated back to 1980, when I was asked to chair one of the plenary sessions at a conference in Edinburgh, Scotland, celebrating the 70th anniversary of the 1910 World Missions gathering, a pivotal moment in the history of world missions.

While I was speaking, a missionary to Greenland—a young Swedish man named Erik Stadell—unexpectedly came up to the platform and asked to say a word, which I allowed. I cannot remember everything he said during his brief appearance, but he concluded with a dramatic rallying cry that he shouted several times: "A church for every people by the year 2000!" As he continued to bellow this phrase—one none of us had heard before—we were unsure how to handle his intervention, and some began to feel uncomfortable. In the weeks and months following the conference, his challenge lingered in my mind and heart, and I felt the Lord had used this man to launch something dynamic.

After Thomas Wang became the director of the Lausanne Movement in 1987, he embraced this challenge of establishing a church for every people by 2000. He widely publicized this catchphrase, urging the body of Christ to seize the opportunity and launch a major initiative to reach the unevangelized peoples of the world. Shortly thereafter, a group of people met and agreed to form a leadership team to advance this vision. The AD2000 Movement was born with a sense of destiny to take up the challenge, focusing specifically on the decade of the 1990s.

Argentina-born Luis Bush was invited to serve as the international director of the new movement. He approached many mission leaders, encouraging them to do everything possible to achieve the ambitious goal of establishing a church among every people group by the year 2000. He asked John Robb and me to co-lead the Unreached Peoples Track. Other key figures included John Bendor-Samuel (Wycliffe Bible Translators), George Verwer (Operation Mobilization), Roger Forster (March For Jesus), Peter and Doris Wagner (Prayer), Paul Eshleman (Campus Crusade and the Jesus Film), Phill Butler (Partnering), and Jim Engel (Strategy). Nearly all the leaders of the new movement were men already deeply involved in strategizing, mobilizing, and discipling within the mission world. It was an extraordinary assembly of influential activists representing a significant proportion of the world's missionary force.

As the dynamic movement began to take shape, the catchphrase was modified to: "A church for every people and the gospel for every person by the year 2000." This broadened the vision to include evangelism and church planting, better reflecting the Lord's command to disciple the nations. Meanwhile, the name of the movement was adjusted to the "AD2000 and Beyond Movement" to avoid implying that we expected the goals to be fully reached by the year 2000, along with all the accompanying eschatological implications. However, as we later found out, the final decade of the twentieth century saw the largest ingathering of individuals and the greatest expansion of the church that the world has ever seen. I estimate that more than 140 million people were added to the body of Christ during that decade. While not all these conversions can be attributed to this movement, I have no doubt that a considerable proportion of those salvations were directly or indirectly due to the focus brought by the AD2000 and Beyond initiative.

Luis Bush is credited with coining the term, "10/40 Window," which entered the lexicon of millions of Christians for the first time in history. The 10/40 Window refers to the area between the Atlantic and Pacific Oceans across Africa and Asia, lying between 10 degrees and 40 degrees latitude north of the Equator. This rectangular "window" encompasses the vast majority of the world's least evangelized people. Luis promoted the concept widely, leading thousands of churches and ministries to refocus their efforts on the least evangelized. While the 10/40 Window concept stimulated much interest, it oversimplified the unfinished task. Geographically, it left out large unreached areas and populations, such as Central Asia, Mongolia, Indonesia, Somalia, Mozambique, Comoros, and many countries bordering the Indian Ocean. On the other hand, the window included regions that already had high densities of Christians, including South Korea, northeastern India, parts of China, and Nigeria and Chad in Africa. It also led to many downgrading the value of efforts to evangelize areas outside the 10/40 Window.

Before the AD2000 and Beyond Movement was formed, many good mission agencies were involved in the Great Commission, but little synergy existed among groups from different denominational backgrounds. Each ministry tended to pursue its own vision. Furthermore, countless churches and missions focused solely on reaching lost individuals. It didn't matter if those individuals were in the Philippines, Alabama, or Timbuktu—a lost soul was a lost soul. This is evangelism, and there are lost individuals in every community on earth. Many missionaries have been told while visiting home, "There are plenty of lost souls right here, so we don't need to go overseas."

While it is true that there are needs everywhere, the AD2000 and Beyond Movement elevated and clarified the focus. The goal was not only to reach unsaved individuals but to see entire segments of humanity reached for Jesus Christ—often groups that had never heard his name before. To do this required faith, courage, and boldness, as well as a specific focus and targeted strategies. By concentrating on identifying and reaching the world's unevangelized peoples, a great number of ministries were able to unite and find common ground in Christ around a single vision. As a result, many ideas and resources were shared, adding momentum to the global missionary movement.

We held several global conferences that shaped and promoted this vision. The first was held in 1995 in Seoul, South Korea, where 70,000 young Koreans filled the Seoul Olympic Stadium. It was during that conference that the first Korean edition of *Operation World* was launched. Many of the approximately 12,000 Korean missionaries mobilized by the start of the new millennium credited their calling or field selection to this book.

As part of the myriad initiatives spurred by the movement, the Joshua Project was launched in 1995 under the leadership of Dan Scribner. This remarkable ministry quickly became the go-to place on the internet for anyone seeking information about the peoples and languages of the world. It hosted the first publicly available list of all major ethnolinguistic groups, becoming an essential tool for implementing the vision of a church for every people.

Over time, the information provided by the Joshua Project surpassed the data many governments had on their own countries. This made some political leaders feel insecure, leading to accusations that the ministry was a well-financed arm of the US government or a tool of Western imperialism. However, the reality was quite different. To this day, the Joshua Project operates on a shoestring budget, supported by a small team of mission-minded Christians passionate about seeing God's kingdom come on earth as it is in heaven. At one point, the president of a small Asian country even blamed the Joshua Project for his election defeat, claiming that the information on their website had destabilized his re-election campaign.

As the persistent message of advocating for the least reached continued to be proclaimed throughout the 1990s, many new global and regional conferences were organized, resulting in new initiatives and recruits for missions, especially in Africa, Asia, and Latin America. Ministries also reported an increase in the number of workers focusing on the more-evangelized countries in Europe, North America, and the Pacific.

In a move that some found surprising, shortly after our launch in 1991, I was partly responsible for a push to commit to closing the Movement in the year 2000. I was aware that many movements can easily self-perpetuate beyond their maximum impact time, which can hinder the emergence of a new generation of relevant and dynamic initiatives. We didn't want to create an organization that would last for generations; our role was to sound a trumpet and call God's people to action for a specific task, which would eventually be completed.

We fully realized that it was unlikely we would achieve our goal of a church for every people and the gospel for every person by 2000. New initiatives would be needed. I believe the primary role of the Movement was to sharpen focus to the global church on the long-neglected need to disciple the nations (ethnic groups) of the world and to start fires that would be taken up and spread further by believers targeting the most unreached. I believe this goal was also achieved, as tens of thousands of pastors and ministry leaders across the world began incorporating terms like "unreached people groups" into their lexicon for the first time.

We kept our commitment to close the AD2000 and Beyond Movement at the end of 2000, but sadly it occurred in a way we weren't expecting. We had planned a great celebration in

Jerusalem at the end of the year, but it had to be canceled at the last moment because of a prolonged strike by Israeli customs and immigration workers.

Looking back, I believe the Lord Jesus Christ accomplished what he intended through the Movement. A new and more strategic course was set in the missions world, which numerous groups have carried on to this day. The AD2000 and Beyond Movement effectively raised a banner with a clear message, inviting any group that desired to march with other believers toward that common goal to join in. Ralph Winter, founder of the US Center for World Mission, called AD2000 "the largest and most pervasive global evangelical network ever to exist." In 2001, we held a conference in Oslo, Norway, where the baton was effectively handed back from the AD2000 and Beyond Movement to the rejuvenated Lausanne Movement.

I will record Rahab and Babylon
among those who acknowledge me—
Philistia too, and Tyre, along with Cush—
and will say, "This one was born in Zion."
The LORD will write in the register of the peoples:
"This one was born in Zion." (Ps 87:4, 6)

In this fascinating passage, we learn that the Lord keeps a "register of the peoples" in heaven. Throughout Scripture, from Genesis to Revelation, we see that our Creator has a clear view of all the nations (ethnic groups) of the world, as demonstrated in the Table of Nations listed in Genesis 10, which immediately precedes the account of their scattering throughout the earth at the Tower of Babel.

At the end of the Bible, we read how the King of kings will have redeemed "a great multitude that no one could count, from every nation, tribe, people, and language" (Rev 7:9). If we fail to complete the task of world evangelization, he has a backup plan. An astonished Apostle John wrote: "Then I saw another angel flying in mid-air, and he had the eternal gospel to proclaim to those who live on the earth—to every nation, tribe, language, and people" (Rev 14:6). While we can rest assured that God maintains a perfect register of all the peoples and languages in the world, how I wish we were allowed to have a copy down here!

As the AD2000 and Beyond Movement gathered momentum in the early 1990s, we faced a crisis. We had committed to planting a church among every people group by the end of 2000. With less than a decade to go, we had no definitive, published list of the world's groups, and we had even less information about their exposure to the gospel. The stated goal of the movement, "A church for every people and the gospel for every person by the year 2000," was unattainable without a credible list of the people groups of the world. This became my major task for the remainder of the 1990s.

For years, I had been working with David Barrett on his ethnolinguistic peoples database in collaboration with various mission agencies, deriving information from numerous sources. When I told Luis Bush that I could provide a major sample of the peoples database to help implement the movement's church-planting goal, he was delighted and relieved. To produce a specific listing of unreached peoples, I extracted the names and details of every group with a population of over 10,000 people where less than 5 percent were Christians. This unreached category totaled 1,739 of the 13,000+ names in our database. Of these, we estimated that 539 had no recognizable church within their culture.

In 1997, we published the list in an A4-sized book titled *Global Guide to Unreached Peoples*, which contained all 1,739 peoples arranged in five formats—alphabetically and by country, region, people cluster, and language. Key information on each people group was included, such as the number of Christians and Evangelical believers, the number of denominations and agencies working among them, and the availability of Scripture or gospel audio and video resources, if any, in their languages. I also included a breakdown of each group's affinity bloc and people clusters.

This initial list of 1,739 unreached groups became fundamental to our entire strategy and led to a global adopt-a-people program, which saw large numbers of Christians signing up to pray for and work toward ministry to a specific people group. I'm confident that thousands of new churches were planted among the world's most unreached groups thanks to this initiative.

We could only use the partial list derived from the Barratt database until the publication of the 2001 *World Christian Encyclopedia*. Since then, this original listing of 12,583 ethno-linguistic people groups has given rise to two other main listings: the Southern Baptist International Mission Board and the Joshua Project. These listings have somewhat diverged as new data has emerged, and they have been adapted for more effective application by the networks they serve. The Joshua Project further expanded its listing by replacing the 438 ethno-linguistic peoples of India with nearly 4,000 castes, as this approach is deemed more relevant for effective discipling of all India's peoples. All the people groups are easily accessible on their website: https://joshuaproject.net/.

A further crucial piece in this God-inspired puzzle took shape when the Bethany World Prayer Center in Louisiana committed to writing four-page profiles of all 1,739 unreached groups, including maps, data, and prayer points. Collaborating with over forty ministries, the church invested $450,000 of their budget to complete the task. It took two years and over 50,000 hours of teamwork—but they got it done! Over two million prayer profiles were printed and distributed, and it felt like we had finally added some flesh to the bones of the vision. Multitudes of Christians now had something solid in their hands to help them pray for and go to the unreached peoples of the world.

After the closure of the AD2000 and Beyond Movement in 2001, the Joshua Project continued, and to this day, their small team continues to faithfully track the latest information, refining their data based on input from people on the field. They also incorporate new research as previously unknown people groups are still being "discovered."

As this book was being prepared for publication, the Joshua Project list has evolved and grown significantly. Their website currently lists a total of 17,313 people groups in the world, of which 7,278 are considered "unreached." More than 3.4 billion people live in those lost groups, so the task is still far from complete. However, I know the situation would have been much worse today if not for the God-given vision for unreached peoples that I have been privileged to be involved with through the AD2000 and Beyond Movement and the Joshua Project.

23

1993—
OPERATION WORLD 5

After losing Jill, I returned to the huge task of completing the next edition of *Operation World*—the fifth edition, not counting all the revisions along the way. I had a difficult time adjusting. Each edition of *Operation World* has had its death points, moments when we reach rock bottom and wonder if we will ever make it to the end. On each occasion, we have clung to the promises of God, and only then has his resurrection power carried us through to the finish line. This time, my struggle was compounded by a literal death accompanied by grief and deep pain.

The Lord blessed us with the arrival of John and Margaret Bardsley, whom I met during a speaking tour in Western Australia in 1988. This remarkable couple had served in Indonesia before becoming the WEC representatives in Perth. They suspended their lives in Australia and moved with their three daughters to England to assist me. John was a gifted public speaker with many abilities, while Margaret was an excellent secretary and personal assistant.

By this time, I had completed the draft text for about two-thirds of the countries in the world. Our local mailman's bag was heavy with letters each day, as drafts were sent overseas for checking and corrections were returned from respondents. Email was still in its infancy, but Margaret did an amazing job juggling all these responsibilities.

Some significant additions to the 1993 edition included our first global assessment of Charismatics and Pentecostals across the Christian church. We assessed the estimated percentage of Charismatics in every denomination from 1960 to 1990. When we finally tallied the worldwide numbers, our totals were very close to those calculated by the *World Christian Encyclopedia* team, who used their own methodology. This was an encouraging confirmation of our methodologies.

For the first time, an electronic version of *Operation World* was pioneered by Global Mapping International (GMI). After two years of collaboration, Mike O'Rear of GMI and his brilliant team produced a CD containing the full range of our diagrams, maps, databases, and other information that was too extensive to fit into a printed book.

We also published approximate figures for how many cross-cultural missionaries each country had received and sent out, provided those figures didn't compromise the security of ministries or individuals. This marked the first serious survey of the global missionary force since the early twentieth century.

Again, we relied heavily on information from evangelical missions around the world. Almost every ministry enthusiastically assisted us, although one large mission organization with more than 1,000 missionaries failed to respond to repeated requests for their statistics. I eventually wrote to their international director, informing him that if we didn't have their statistics, we would remove every mention of their ministry from the book. By this time, the status of *Operation World* was such that we received a quick response with all their relevant statistics!

Another ministry, which specialized in producing and distributing audio Scripture in thousands of languages and dialects, had an internal dispute over policy that resulted in a major split between their national bodies, who then decided to form their own independent missions. When we listed missions in *Operation World*, we always included sub-ministries under the overall mission agency name. This group now insisted that we list them as separate entities in the 1993 edition. I responded that if they insisted, I would remove all reference to their work from the book. This shock treatment forced them to rethink, resulting in the emergence of a cooperative network of national agencies under the title of "Global Recordings." We were thus able to encourage a reconciliation through our leverage with *Operation World*.

The fall of the Iron Curtain in 1989 and the subsequent collapse of the Soviet Union resulted in the formation of sixteen new independent states. This created a huge challenge for us, as information about the religious composition of these new countries was scarce. Using every scrap of information we could find about each country, we distributed the overall USSR figures for the registered and unregistered Baptists, Mennonites, Pentecostals, and others across the sixteen new nations. We found there was no point in asking our sources within these countries, because the local church leaders didn't know the specifics either. We published our estimates, and years later, I discovered that local believers in those countries were relying on my estimates from the Russian edition of *Operation World* because they had no better information.

After a long struggle to reach the finish line, in April 1993 we submitted two books—*Operation World* and *You Can Change the World*—to OM Publishing for printing and to Global Mapping for producing the electronic versions. Many other products were also made available, such as prayer cards and maps. Much of the good publicity was generated by the tireless George Verwer, who remained passionate about promoting the book and giving away thousands of copies. These factors combined to make the 1993 edition one of our most successful, with translations published in at least twenty-four languages.

Meanwhile, Daphne and Rosie did a great job with the second volume of *You Can Change the World*, both before and after Jill's death. It was published alongside the 1993 edition of *Operation World*, with similar cover illustrations, which helped the publisher market both books as a set. Later, both volumes were merged and updated by Daphne and published with the 2001 edition of *Operation World* under the title *Window on the World*.

In the months leading up to the publication of a book, I was always extremely busy. However, after finishing the 1993 edition, I took a breather as I was still going through a difficult grieving process following Jill's loss. I felt I needed to take time to process everything that had happened, recharge my batteries, and make necessary adjustments in my life and ministries. My WEC colleagues graciously granted me a four-month sabbatical.

Lying on a beach or playing golf for an extended period is not my idea of relaxation. Instead, I headed to Richmond, Virginia, where I received a warm welcome from David Barrett and the *World Christian Encyclopedia* team. The experience proved to be everything that I could have dreamed of in helping me recover, as I handled statistics and engaged in intense brainstorming sessions about world evangelization. Many close friendships were formed that proved productive for the kingdom of God.

Todd Johnson had joined the *World Christian Encyclopedia* team four years earlier, after many years with Youth With A Mission. Todd is an eminently gifted researcher and ultimately succeeded David Barrett as head of the organization. He and his wife Trish (the daughter of Ralph and Roberta Winter) became good friends. I admired Todd's skills in dealing with the forceful personalities of two giants of the mission world—his leader, David Barrett, and his father-in-law, Ralph Winter. Both men had strong opinions and posed challenges to everyone who worked with them. Todd's wisdom and diplomatic skills impressed me, as he maintained good relationships with both Barrett and Winter for years.

For many years, *Operation World* and the *World Christian Encyclopedia* had maintained separate databases, employing slightly different methodologies and definitions in analyzing Christian statistics and quantifying the remaining task of world evangelization. During my sabbatical, we had many fruitful discussions, which enabled us to align our statistics as closely as our sources and principles would allow. This facilitated fair comparisons of our respective data, leading to a considerable degree of confirmation of our separate research findings.

One shared statistical principle, referred to as "The 100 percent rule" by both of our teams, is something we constantly affirm. Essentially, this rule states that the total for every component of a selected set of statistics *must* add up to 100 percent. If it does not, we have either made a mistake in our assumptions or data, or there is a valid reason for the discrepancy that must be accounted for. For example, if we provide a breakdown of a country's religious affiliations, the total of all that country's religions must equal 100 percent of the population. This approach allows us to address issues such as double counting, secret believers, and religious nominalism without exceeding the total.

During one discussion, I mentioned to David and Todd that we could use the database to produce a list of all the nomadic and partially nomadic peoples in the world. David initially responded that this was impossible, but I assured him that we could do it. I then accessed the database, and within minutes, I had completed the task and presented a printout of the list. Much of David's computer-related work had been delegated to others, so I think he had not fully grasped the vast range of possible applications for the collected data. Todd was instrumental in helping transition their team to the digital age.

I thank God for David Barrett, Todd Johnson, and their colleagues for the years spent working together in Christian research. They have made a great contribution to the global church's efforts to make disciples of all nations. David went to his eternal reward in 2011 at the age of 84, but the collaboration between Todd and the *Operation World* team continues to this day.

I took my list of nomadic people groups back with me to the United Kingdom. One of our team members, David Phillips, was an invaluable support to me as a sifter of vital information for the text and data of *Operation World*. After I dropped the list on his desk, he became so enthusiastic that he undertook to write a book on the world's nomads. *Peoples on the Move* became the standard reference for nomads and Christian ministry among them.

David Garrison of the International Mission Board first explored grouping as a means of organizing all peoples and languages into major blocs, such as the Arab and Turkic worlds, Tibeto-Burmans, and others. I expanded on this during my time in Richmond and was able to assign every people group in the database to one of about 250 distinct clusters and one of fifteen major affinity blocs. This helped illustrate how the myriad array of people groups throughout the world are related. In many cases, the gospel could spread more easily between people groups that share a common history, culture, or language. Mobilizing missionaries from a people group that shares those commonalities could potentially advance the kingdom of God more quickly than sending outsiders from completely different backgrounds.

In the new year, I traveled to Urbana, Illinois, to speak at the large biennial student mission conference. While there, I received news that Norman Grubb, the first WEC leader after C. T. Studd, had died in Philadelphia. I was able to drive to the funeral and honor the man whose ministry had so profoundly impacted my life. I returned to England in February 1994 feeling well-rested and eager to embark on the next phase of my life.

24

Robyn

After the wonderful, strategic break I enjoyed in the United States, I returned to my busy life at Bulstrode. For the previous three years, I had limited my travel due to Jill's illness and my commitment to completing the 1993 edition of *Operation World*. This caused a considerable backlog of invitations for me to minister around the world, which could have filled my diary for the next several years.

I had to learn to balance my ministry commitments with being a single parent to three children who were now young adults. Peter, my eldest, found his life partner, Julie, at Bristol University, and we celebrated their wedding at Bulstrode in June 1993. By this time, Peter's attempts to join the Royal Air Force had ended after he was twice turned down during the officer acceptance training phase. I have often wondered if part of the reason was his willingness to openly share his faith in Jesus. He then became a high school math teacher, while Julie was nearing the completion of her training as a medic. At that time, Tim was again serving on the OM ship *MV Doulos* in Asia and Australia, while Ruth was splitting her time between university and our home at Bulstrode.

After Jill's death in 1992, I traveled to South Africa to speak at the 50th anniversary of the founding of the Dorothea Mission. I was delighted to see many of my old colleagues, but after the death of Hans von Staden in 1986 at the age of 81, the mission had been in a slow decline, finding it difficult to replace Hans as its leader. It was a momentous and extraordinary period in South African history, with intense negotiations underway between the races about the possibility of a democratic, multi-racial South Africa. A new draft constitution had just been published, and all apartheid laws had been rescinded. A fully democratic election was planned for 1994.

During my trip to South Africa, I renewed contact with an acquaintance from Bulawayo whose husband had died several years earlier. I sensed her interest in me, and after several encounters with others, I realized that I had to come to terms with the fact that people now perceived me as an eligible widower. The prospect of another relationship left me feeling cautious and vulnerable.

My marriage to Jill had been such a blessed one that I thought no one could ever fill her shoes. However, we had agreed that, should the Lord take one of us, the other would be free to remarry. So, while there were no restrictions on my remarrying, I needed to be certain of God's leading. I was content to remain single, realizing that my lifestyle would make it extremely difficult for anyone to come alongside me.

After Jill died, my daughter Ruth was a wonderful companion and support—she was the only one of my children still living at home. After a while, however, I sensed that she was concerned I might become too dependent on her. She went through the entire list of WEC workers in our personnel book, and of those she knew, she could only think of one suitable person for me: Robyn Erwin, who had been such an answer to prayer in 1989 when Jill needed a coworker.

Among Robyn's many gifts, she played the flute beautifully. At the thanksgiving service for Jill, she had performed a lovely piece. One of the members of our house group leaned over to her husband and whispered, "That is the one Patrick will marry!" She only told me this after Robyn and I began our journey together toward marriage. We later discovered that many other Christians had drawn the same conclusion, which gave us confidence that God was guiding us when we went through difficult times.

Robyn had joined the WEC research office on a two-year commitment to work closely with Jill. My contact with her had been quite fleeting due to my travel schedule and the fact that my office was in a separate part of the Bulstrode complex. As her two-year period was about to expire, Robyn was making plans to work with WEC in Bulgaria among the Turkish-speaking population there. I asked her to consider staying in England a few months longer until we completed both Jill's book and the latest *Operation World*, which she kindly agreed to do.

In late 1992, Robyn arrived in Istanbul to learn Turkish. During her year of language study, at least one colleague in our mission brought up the subject of a possible marriage between us, prompting a stern plea from Robyn to never raise the issue again. In late 1993, I sent two of the first copies of *Operation World* and *You Can Change the World* to Robyn, thanking her for the key role she had played in helping them become a reality. After receiving the books, Robyn replied with a warm chatty letter, and we began to correspond. Being overly optimistic, I read more into this than Robyn had intended.

Eventually, I plucked up the courage to write to Robyn, asking if she would be willing to take our relationship a bit further. Here we ran into a cultural problem! I had deliberately phrased my question in a way that gave her ample room to decline by asking, "Would you be open to considering the possibility of . . ." but she later told me that she felt my choice of words was subtly coercive. How could she point-blank say, "No, I'm not willing to be open!"?

I didn't realize that Robyn had moved to another part of Istanbul, so my letter sat undelivered for several weeks at her old address. In the meantime, I became increasingly concerned about her lack of response, so I sent her a copy of the original letter with a few extra words of encouragement. Both letters eventually reached Robyn within hours of each other, which placed a lot of pressure on her. She consulted her prayer partner, Sharon, who knew both of us and was excited about the development! Sharon is South African, and as a young woman, had been discipled by Jill when we lived in Bulawayo.

Meanwhile, I traveled to the United States for a special WEC leadership meeting, where I reported on our mission's progress and made suggestions for our future. I proposed taking time to fully absorb all the stresses and strains from the massive changes our ministry structures had experienced since the launch of the STEP program ten years before. The previous decade of harvest had precipitated explosive growth in the number of new WEC workers on the mission field. I felt that if our ministry set aside a period to reflect on everything that had happened, it would give us time to prepare a new vision and to set goals, ensuring that everything would be in place for an impactful start to our next major push forward. Therefore, I proposed that we prepare thoroughly for a new initiative in AD 2000, in line with WEC's sixteen-year pattern of renewal.

My proposals were mostly accepted, but my suggested timeline to begin the new initiative in 2000 was rejected; I was asked to schedule a launch date in 1996. That was a mere two years away. My heart sank as I recalled that our previous advance in 1984 had required at least four years to prepare all our ministries for an effective launch. In retrospect, I believe my reasoning and proposals to the WEC leaders were valid, and the subsequent launch in 1996 was poorly executed because we were unable to fully invest the time and effort needed to successfully implement our strategy in such a short timeframe.

As this upheaval unfolded in the United States, Robyn called me from Turkey. Despite her shock at receiving my two letters just a few hours apart, she felt concerned and wanted to reassure me that she had received them. This led to daily phone conversations between us, interspersed with WEC leadership meetings and planning sessions. Due to of her situation as part of a mission team in Istanbul, Robyn felt she should confide in her team leaders, Mike and Deanne O'Donnell. Mike asked Robyn, "Has he proposed to you?" to which she responded negatively. When she recounted this to me the next day during our call, I impulsively asked, "If I had asked you to marry me, what would your response have been?" Robyn replied, "Yes." The issue was decided for me far earlier than I had expected!

A few days later, Robyn's Turkish language teacher challenged her students to share in Turkish about their most exciting day. Robyn chose to share what had transpired between us in her limited Turkish. The teacher was not a Christian, but nearly all the students were believers, with most being part of our organization. As Robyn developed the story, everyone in the room hung on her words. The teacher soon realized that the man in Robyn's story was known to nearly all her classmates. The secret was out, and it quickly spread like wildfire throughout the WEC family.

Considering our impending marriage, Robyn decided it was pointless to continue her Turkish language studies, although she had enjoyed the experience. Next, we faced the challenge of navigating my busy travel schedule, as we struggled to find a time to be together in the same country to arrange our wedding and lay a foundation for our marriage.

25

The Tour from Hell

I am too much of an optimist, always believing that things will turn out well. I had a deep peace in my heart that the Lord would work things out for Robyn and me. This optimism, combined with a strong sense of loyalty to those who lead or ask things of me, has profoundly affected the people closest to me through the ministry patterns I embraced.

During my marriage to Jill, we shared similar characteristics, which meant she did not challenge the hidden areas in my life that needed to be addressed. Now as I was preparing for marriage with Robyn—an introvert who values a low profile and cherishes time alone with God—some friends and colleagues expressed concern about her committing to the express train called Patrick and wondered how we would manage. By God's grace, we did manage, but it was a long learning experience for both of us. I needed someone like Robyn to disciple me and help me confront my hidden baggage, and on the other side of the coin, perhaps I, too, have been used by the Lord to help her find new freedom in Jesus.

One of our first major challenges was fitting our wedding and honeymoon into my packed travel schedule. In addition to other international trips, I had long-planned speaking tours in Central and South America, Scotland, and Northern Ireland in late 1994, followed by Spain in December. Then from March to May, I would be traveling to Australia, New Zealand, and South Korea, with South Africa scheduled for August and September

1995. As a result, everything had to be squeezed into an already full calendar for the coming years.

Robyn and I managed to spend valuable time together in England before I left for an eight-week trip to Brazil and Mexico, and before she went to California to spend time with family and friends at her home church. As my tour of Latin America progressed, Robyn and I wrote to each other almost daily. Although we were months away from standing together at the altar, it became clear that Robyn was seriously wondering how she could cope with my ministry lifestyle. It became essential for us to spend quality time together, so I changed my flights and flew from Mexico to Philadelphia to spend valuable days with Robyn at the WEC USA headquarters. She later came to Bulstrode to spend more undistracted time with me as we scheduled our wedding for February 4, 1995.

To make matters more challenging, both my son Tim and daughter Ruth found life partners and were planning their own weddings! Ruth was scheduled to marry Andy Bull at the end of 1994, and soon after, Tim got engaged to a girl from New Zealand, planning to hold their wedding there.

By consensus, we decided that Ruth and Andy would get married in December, Robyn and I would wed in the United States in early February, and finally, Tim would tie the knot in New Zealand in late February or early March. Fitting everything together felt like playing Tetris! Our plan included having our honeymoon in New Zealand before Tim's wedding, after which we would continue to Australia for the beginning of my scheduled speaking tour.

We all got busy planning our three weddings within a three-month period, and our little apartment at Bulstrode became crowded with three engaged couples for several weeks in December. Just as everything seemed poised to come together, Tim's fiancée broke off the engagement, and the wedding was canceled. By this time, everyone (including my mother and sister) had already bought tickets to America and New Zealand, so we all decided not to change our travel plans.

Robyn and I flew into a snowy Philadelphia, where our WEC USA colleagues warmly welcomed us. Our wedding went smoothly, and we flew on to New Zealand, where friends had arranged a wonderful "bach" (holiday cottage) and a vehicle for our honeymoon on the Coromandel Peninsula. My mother used the time to enjoy a bus tour of New Zealand, while my sister Caroline, with support from her husband, completed a 1,250-mile (2,000 km) sponsored bicycle ride from the very tip of North Island down to Bluff at the bottom of the picturesque South Island.

Neil and Mary Rowe were our first WEC leaders after Jill and I moved back to the United Kingdom. Mary passed away from cancer in 1988, and two years later, Neil married Jackie, a fellow WEC worker. Someone told Neil before the wedding, "This will be a new chapter in your life!" to which he replied, "No. It will be a new book!" That is how I would describe it too.

God has blessed me with two remarkable life partners. Each is quite different from the other, yet both have been greatly used by the Holy Spirit to mold and shape me. Life often feels like peeling an onion layer by layer—including all the tears! Jill and Robyn have been two great discipling influences on me. When Robyn entered my life, the Lord used her to help me deal with yet more layers of my life-onion that had previously been hidden from view. Deep down, I still didn't recognize that I had an issue with overcommitting to people and ministries. This imbalance ultimately caused pain to my family.

After our honeymoon, we went straight into an extensive seven-week speaking tour of Australia followed by two weeks in New Zealand. I had left the planning of our Australian itinerary to our WEC representatives in each state, and due to everything else going on, I hadn't paid close attention to the schedule being developed for us. The Australians had asked John Bardsley what kinds of things I enjoyed, and he replied, "Patrick loves meetings, so fill up his schedule!"

We were assigned to spend one week in each Australian state, with the seventh day reserved for traveling to the next state. With a program that included two or three meetings per day, there was no time to rest or reflect. I survived, but the impact on my new bride was devastating. In the years that followed, she referred to the trip as the "tour from hell."

After our tour in Australia and New Zealand, I flew straight to South Korea to be one of the main speakers at the AD2000 and Beyond Global Conference on World Evangelization. Robyn had intended to fly to California to spend time with family and friends while I was in Korea, but the trip had been so exhausting that she left halfway through the New Zealand leg of the tour.

In total, we spoke at about 140 meetings over nine weeks. It was only later that I began to understand how awful this experience had been to Robyn. I urgently needed to do a major overhaul of my boundaries and future ministry. I was deeply grieved that, in my over-optimism, I had selfishly burdened my distraught wife. Although God used those months of speaking to call people into missions, I resolved never to go on a speaking tour like that again. Robyn and I agreed that she would accompany me only if there was some direct involvement in ministry that suited her giftings.

Back in the United Kingdom, when Robyn and I were planning our future together, she said that it would be wonderful to start our married life away from the goldfish bowl of life at Bulstrode. That thought had never crossed my mind because we simply didn't have the money to put down a deposit on a house and pay a mortgage. We had lived by trusting the Lord and had no regular or guaranteed income. Consequently, no financial institution would ever consider giving us a mortgage based on our faith.

As I mentioned previously, sometimes I heard of people who assumed I was a millionaire due to the success of *Operation World*. That always elicited a wry smile from me because the income from the book was reinvested into the cost of researching and writing the next edition as well as financing new projects. The bulk of the royalties from *Operation World* were placed into a Christian trust that invested the money, and from this balance, we could request funds for ministry needs and office expenses.

One day, unexpectedly, the leader of the trust mentioned that we might need to buy a house and asked if we would be willing to receive a loan from the *Operation World* holdings to put down a deposit on a home. He assured us that the loan could be paid back gradually as we were able. We gladly accepted this suggestion and successfully found a little terrace (row) house in the West London suburb of Hillingdon.

We were thankful for a place to call our own, and later we understood how providential the timing of this offer and purchase had been. Robyn and I traveled to the British Consulate in New York to obtain a visa for her to enter the United Kingdom as my wife. The process was much more complicated than we expected. Due to the long history of abuse of this method by smugglers and illegal immigrant networks, the UK had very strict rules regarding British husbands bringing foreign brides into the country. We had to prove the legality of our marriage and demonstrate that I was able to provide for my wife. As a missionary, I had no evidence of a steady income, but because we were now the joint owners of a house, we were able to satisfy the requirements, and Robyn was granted a resident visa. Years later, she became a citizen of the United Kingdom.

We repaid the loan over the next seven years. During that time, house prices rose sharply and we were able to sell what had been an £80,000 house for £180,000. What a blessing that has been to us throughout our married life! Later, when we moved to other parts of the country, we were not burdened by a mortgage.

We settled into new work routines. Increasingly, Robyn took on more of an administrative role, and although she felt this was not her gifting, she courageously persevered. Before long, I found myself busy again with my triple ministry responsibilities of writing, leading, and speaking around the world. Due to my hectic schedule, I struggled to focus on my personal issues and shortcomings, which negatively impacted Robyn. At the same time, she was facing feelings of rejection and insignificance, leading both of us to an extended phase of survival mode, grappling with internal issues that we could no longer ignore. By the grace of God, we continued to seek him, and we were blessed during the times when our Heavenly Father revealed himself to us in fresh ways, helping us experience greater freedom as our relationship with him and with each other grew closer.

26

THE CHURCH IS BIGGER THAN YOU THINK

One of my greatest pleasures in public ministry around the world has been witnessing firsthand how the global church has risen to meet the many opportunities presented to it. The church is much larger than most Christians realize. During a speaking tour of Northern Ireland and Scotland, Robyn suggested I write a book on this subject. The idea launched me into a new project that took several years to complete, culminating in a new book titled *The Church Is Bigger than You Think*.

The book title conveys a threefold message I longed to share with the body of Christ. First, I wanted believers everywhere to know that the church spans centuries and cultures. Despite many Christians feeling disheartened by the apparent failings of the church, both past and present, I wanted to show that God's people have always been central to his eternal plan for the redemption of creation.

Second, the church is bigger in size. The astonishing growth of Christianity in the latter part of the twentieth century did not receive the publicity it deserved. This growth was strongest in Latin America, Africa, and many parts of Asia. Consequently, many believers in traditional Christian lands had become negative and pessimistic, because all they could see was people embracing secularism, agnosticism, and atheism. There is a tendency for believers to view the world solely through the lens of their own experiences. As Christianity struggled in many parts of the developed world, some believers adopted the false narrative: "If it's not happening here, it can't be happening anywhere." Many were not aware that God was very much alive and actively transforming millions of lives across the world.

Third, the church is bigger in structure. A prevailing theology of the church and its mission had emerged that marginalized vision and the God-given structures needed to fulfill Jesus's last command. God's people must be reminded of the tremendously deep and effective influence the church has had on world history and continues to have today.

The Church Is Bigger than You Think was published in 1998 and proved successful. It also became a textbook for many training institutions and was translated into five languages.

I continued with my itinerant ministry as a WEC leader throughout the remainder of the 1990s. About half of my overseas trips were in response to invitations from WEC bases. Robyn and I traveled together to many countries, with notable trips to South Africa, the United States, and Chad.

A major event for us was the 1996 WEC International Leaders' Conference, where we launched our second advance program, which had been agreed upon in 1994. In our previous growth initiative, launched in 1984, we doubled the size of our church planting force from around 1,000 workers in thirty-three fields to 2,000 workers by 1996. During that time, we also more than doubled the number of countries in which we had ministry. Partially to help facilitate this growth, the International Research Office in Bulstrode expanded over this same time and became a vital source of information for the massive interest in pioneer missions work that characterized the 1990s. One prominent researcher commented that our office housed the largest accessible collection of information on world evangelization.

The 1990s marked the peak of our productivity, with many visitors coming each week for a few hours or days to gather needed information from our collated country folders, microfiche archives, and extensive collection of overhead transparencies. It was a joy for me that all the information we had painstakingly gathered over thousands of hours of work on *Operation World* was serving this dual purpose. However, our entire research structure was destined to change at the turn of the millennium as the internet became the new global storehouse of all information.

The 1990s were the most exciting decade for the expansion of God's kingdom. I traveled overseas for several months each year and spoke in churches throughout the United Kingdom on many weekends when I was home. This was challenging for Robyn, and I had to learn to temper my people-pleasing compulsion that made it almost impossible to say "no" to requests.

As that decade of harvest came to an end, the world had witnessed the greatest numerical increase in Christians at any time in history. Shortly after the start of the new millennium, however, a noticeable cooling in the advance of the gospel was seen in many countries, with much of the church's activity focused on consolidating the gains of the previous decade rather than aggressively pursuing new territories for Christ. Unless these trends dramatically reverse and God brings unprecedented revival before the return of the Lord Jesus, I suspect the 1990s will be remembered as the greatest decade of harvest in Christian history.

One reason for my pessimistic outlook on the future is the sharp decline in the global birth rate. Most new Christians in the 1990s were children and teenagers. In the future, there will be far fewer young people, with the coming decades likely seeing widespread population collapses and an increasing need to care for the mushrooming elderly population. This demographic shift promises to impact many countries like a tsunami. Its effects are already being felt.

By the end of the twentieth century, seeds of discontent and chaos were already starting to sprout around the world. Jihadist Islam had emerged, declaring war against the West and many Middle Eastern states. The seismic catastrophes of the early twenty-first century soon followed, beginning with 9/11 and its aftermath. Ultimately, it may be said that the end of the millennium saw the curtain drawn on the traditional methods of the 200-year-long, Western-inspired missionary enterprise. The global mission force of the twenty-first century is markedly different and needs to find innovative methods to effectively serve Jesus in more hostile and dangerous environments.

As the year 2000 approached, the millennial year had a special appeal for statisticians, providing a gilt-edged opportunity to make use of millennial, centurial, and decadal totals. Consequently, our team at *Operation World* collaborated with David Barrett and his colleagues at *World Christian Encyclopedia* to plan millennial editions of our respective books.

Both David and I were committed to handling facts and statistics with integrity, but we used differing networks of informants and served distinct readerships. Over the years, we interacted closely regarding the categories and classifications we used to ensure our publications were both compatible and comparable. We also adopted each other's methodologies as much as possible without compromising our data or offending our networks. Despite our varied sources and methods, it was deeply gratifying that our overall results were similar and well within the margins of error in which we operated.

In the late 1990s, David and I were in constant communication through voluminous correspondence and frequent phone calls. We agreed to disagree about David's decision to change the definition of "Evangelicals" in his upcoming *World Christian Encyclopedia*. Since 1977, we had agreed to use the definition of Evangelicals that had emerged from the Lausanne Movement, which was basically theological and experiential. This definition encompassed Christians who believe in the inspiration of Scripture, the atoning work of Christ, the proclamation of salvation, and the need to be born again. This common understanding meant that David and I produced similar figures from our different networks, resulting in compatible statistics understood by our main readership.

But then, David decided unilaterally to add a historical component to his definition: Evangelicals would be defined only as those within historic Protestantism. So in one fell swoop, he excluded most of the indigenous bodies of believers. This meant that millions of believers in large African, Asian, and Latino indigenous churches were no longer counted as Evangelicals unless they were part of a church that identified itself with traditional Protestant labels, such as Methodist, Presbyterian, Baptist, or Lutheran.

Tens of millions of Christians in China, for example, were no longer considered Evangelical despite being in the midst of one of the greatest revivals in Christian history. Ironically, experts on the Chinese church noted how the Lord Jesus used the persecution of the church by the Communist authorities and pressures to cut all links, including denominational labels, with foreign bodies and thus laid the groundwork for China's great revival. Those believers in China and many other parts of the world were disciples of the Lord who cared little about the church background of the missionary who first brought the gospel to them a century or more ago.

I believe that most of us involved in missionary work and discipleship want to know one simple reality—who our fellow believers are that preach the same fundamental gospel message. By making his decision without adequate consultation with the wider Evangelical community, David's publications, in my opinion, became less useful and incompatible with how we presented and enumerated the body of Christ in *Operation World*. I believe David's decision was a mistake, as it brought confusion to many who wanted consistency.

Some months later, while completing the statistics and text for a group of countries, I requested the next batch of David's data so we could incorporate it as much as possible into our books as we had agreed. His response was distressing. David insisted that he would only share his data if I agreed to use it without making any adjustments. This condition, of course, was not possible as I could not with integrity alter the vast quantity of sourced data we had collected to align with his figures. Making such changes would have disrespected the hundreds of informants who had supplied us with data that the *World Christian Encyclopedia* team did not have. Despite much discussion by phone, David remained adamant. I had so hoped that a measure of convergence within our margins of error would go a long way to affirm our respective works and the meticulous research we had done using different information networks. Thus, this marked the end of our personal interactions as we moved toward publication for both projects.

I treasure my many years of cooperation with David and admire the remarkable giftings God placed in his life. His tireless devotion to Christian research had reportedly taken him to 212 of the 223 recognized countries in the world, enabling him to form a vast network of contacts. His brilliant mind gave birth to the first comprehensive list of the world's religions, denominations, people groups, and the study of two millennia of Christian martyrs. He also published the first list of the world's languages categorized by their relationships to one another. The Operation World team and the World Christian Encyclopedia team resumed close cooperation for subsequent editions.

27

2001—
OPERATION WORLD 6

After our June 1996 WEC Leaders' Conference, my focus shifted to preparing for the sixth edition of *Operation World*. Each previous edition had been a major undertaking requiring three to four years of research and writing.

First, we needed to rebuild our informant networks and gather additional information from both secular and religious sources to further develop our database, which was the heartbeat of all our information. Given the expanding needs of the computer age in an ever-changing world, we needed to gather a new team with the appropriate skills. Since we were a team of unpaid volunteers, we had to pray in each team member. What answers to prayer we had! At times, I stood back in amazement as God brought a myriad of people with diverse gifts and personalities to our door. I had a little glimpse of how Noah must have felt as God supernaturally directed the animals to the ark! Like a train gradually gaining momentum as it pulls away from the station, my personal involvement with the sixth edition steadily increased, until it consumed most of my time during its last two years of production. As usual, much of my writing was done in the early morning or evenings.

The way *Operation World* has been produced over three decades has undergone enormous change. I compiled the first three editions in Africa, working alone. The 1986, 1993, and 2001 editions were then assembled in our research office at Bulstrode, with each successive edition seeing an increase in the number of volunteers working on it. I look back in awe, amazed at how each person came as a special gift of grace from the Lord. Because we didn't employ any workers, the atmosphere was very different from environments with salaried staff who can be hired and fired. Some tremendously competent people joined us, while others learned tasks they had never dreamed of and had to be practically spoon-fed until they got used to their roles.

With this edition, a key challenge was to ensure the book did not become too large. The 1978 edition had 267 pages, the 1986 edition contained 500 pages, and the 1993 edition ballooned to 662 pages. I struggled to keep the page count below 800 for this sixth edition, which we hoped to release in time for the new millennium. While we did succeed in limiting the number of pages to fewer than 800, we completed the book a year later than planned.

The 2001 edition featured several significant improvements, including an "Answers to Prayer" section. As I looked back at earlier editions, I noticed that many of the previous prayer points had already been answered. Thus, we decided to precede each country's prayer requests with specific answers that God had provided in the past. This encouraged readers and inspired faith in those embarking on a life of intercession.

Some of the amazing answers to prayer we had seen included: the collapse of Communism in Europe and the opening to the gospel of the former Soviet Bloc; the largely peaceful ending of apartheid in South Africa; the stunning growth of the church in China; and significant breakthroughs among many previously unreached people groups across major religious systems—first Buddhism, then Hinduism, and more recently throughout the Muslim world.

We were blessed to have the input of Marko Jauhiainen from Finland for much of the programming of our databases, which facilitated the production of the information and graphs we needed. Marko had a doctorate in computer science, which we took full advantage of. After he left us, we benefited from the invaluable help of Maurice Manktelow, a consultant and lecturer in computer sciences. Both Maurice and Marko were able to make our database do extraordinary things!

David Phillips continued in his vital role of reviewing all our files and documents and preparing summary sheets that highlighted important information. David's work saved me many months of research and enabled us to complete the book much more quickly than we otherwise would have. Robyn took on various roles, including editing and typing my handwritten text for each country in the book. At the same time, she found fulfillment in a ministry where she came alongside others and discipled them as they walked with the Lord. Other members of our *Operation World* 2001 "Dream Team" sound like a mini-United Nations roll call! They included Lee Nicholson from New Zealand, Kichul Jeong from South Korea, Terrie Jackson from Australia, and Justine Garner from Britain.

For the first time, key personnel from other mission organizations were temporarily assigned to help us complete the book. They included Darrell Dorr from the US Center for World Mission, who is an expert on the Muslim world, and Michael and Dawna Jaffarian, Baptist missionaries from America with extensive experience in Singapore and as members of David Barrett's *World Christian Encyclopedia* team. Michael helped greatly with the special survey of mission agencies included in the 2001 edition.

Meanwhile, in a key development, a young Canadian named Jason Mandryk joined us and gradually began to assume more responsibility as I prepared him to possibly take over the authorship of future *Operation World* editions. I will share more about Jason in an upcoming chapter, but I insisted that his name appear on the cover of the 2001 edition alongside mine, both to acknowledge his contribution to the book and to demonstrate that a succession plan was in place.

I look back with fond appreciation at the remarkable on-site team God brought together to enable *Operation World: 21st Century Edition* to come into existence. I doubt that such a connected group of people will be gathered in one place again; these days, most teams are virtual, and work is done online. I much prefer the dynamic environment created by personal interactions, the stimulation of ideas, and the discipling processes that occur when people are physically together. How privileged we were!

Normally, when we finish our roles and send the final book files to a publisher, we breathe a huge sigh of relief and sit back with excited anticipation to see the final product when it rolls off the printing press. Alas, on this occasion, the end process was anything but straightforward. We experienced setbacks and a publishing drama before the 2001 edition of *Operation World* finally saw the light of day.

On the publishing side, we had earned such a good reputation for accuracy that the publisher, Paternoster, allowed us to retain complete control of the text's editing. They also trusted us to handle the typesetting in-house. This saved us months of time and allowed us to incorporate last-minute updates just two weeks before the book was printed in Chicago. Apparently, nineteen truckloads of paper were needed to print the sixth edition of *Operation World*.

Pre-publication publicity had been excellent, and a lot of hype surrounded the book's launch, which was to be held in London on board the *MV Doulos* on September 8, 2001, with the North American launch set for a week later in Florida.

While writing this edition, I was acutely aware of the growing threat of Jihadist Islam. I included stern warnings about what I could see as impending disasters involving Pakistan, Afghanistan, and the United States, describing Taliban-ruled Afghanistan as "an open festering wound that is poisoning the world." I also noted that Pakistan's *madrassahs* (Islamic schools) were likely to impact the world, and that the United States needed to prepare for a major terrorist attack. Some challenged these harsh statements, but I did not change a word. Sadly, they turned out to be prophetic.

Jason Mandryk and I were both scheduled to attend the Florida book launch. I had a flight booked for September 14, just three days after the attack on the World Trade Center. It was decided that the book launch should proceed, and I managed to secure a ticket on a flight to Boston, which turned out to be only the second flight to cross the Atlantic Ocean after the post-September 11 aviation shutdown. I was astonished by the panic and fear gripping everyone at Boston's Logan International Airport, with many scheduled flights still grounded because pilots were afraid to fly. I finally reached Florida on the 19th, where I joined Jason and the publishing teams from Paternoster and Operation Mobilization.

Despite the tumultuous circumstances surrounding the book's launch, I feel that the 2001 edition was the best and most widely distributed *Operation World* to date. Unfortunately, we did not know that by the end of the first decade of the twenty-first century, everything in the Christian publishing world would change dramatically. Due to societal changes, the revenues of Christian publishers and bookstores were decimated during the 2010s, with most struggling to stay afloat. The vital distribution networks that had been key to the Christian book world just a few years earlier collapsed as they were forced to compete with Amazon, the rise of the internet, and e-books. Furthermore, the first two decades of the twenty-first century saw a dramatic reduction in Christian reading, mirroring a rapid decline in interest in missions among Western churches.

Handover Time

Everyone involved in Christian ministry for a considerable time eventually faces the question of what to do about succession once they have gone to their eternal reward or become too aged to function properly in their calling. Some ministry leaders shy away from succession, especially those with control issues who think that no one else can possibly fulfill their role effectively. However, the Bible has some clear examples of God-appointed succession. Moses commissioned Joshua as his successor (Deut 31); God commanded Elijah to appoint Elisha as his successor (1 Kgs 19); and in the New Testament, it could be argued that the Lord Jesus himself had a risky succession plan by entrusting the future of the kingdom of God to a dozen young men with an array of personalities, strengths, and weaknesses who were still rough around the edges.

A key verse that has always guided me in discipleship ministry and in thinking about succession is found in the Apostle Paul's remarkable words to Timothy: "You then, my son, be strong in the grace that is in Christ Jesus. And the things you have heard me say in the presence of many witnesses entrust to reliable people who will also be qualified to teach others"

(2 Tim 2:1-2). Paul's words have resonated in my heart since I first arrived in Africa in the early 1960s.

Paul referred to four generations: Paul himself, who taught Timothy, who was to entrust the truth to reliable people, who would in turn pass it on to others. It became my ambition to disciple leaders to a fourth generation, and I desired to hand over as many of my ministry responsibilities to qualified, quality believers as the Lord revealed.

It has been said that every Christian's ambition should be to work themselves out of a job by training their replacement. There is much truth in that sentiment, but over the years, I have seen countless leaders who had no succession plan, resulting in their church or ministry ending when they fell ill or died. Other leaders know they need a successor, but either cannot find anyone they consider good enough or fail to take the task seriously enough and simply run out of time.

Leaders need humility for succession to work. Those who view ministry as their personal fiefdom will have little motivation to seek a replacement. In contrast, those who understand that they are just one part of the body of Christ—and that the Holy Spirit calls and empowers many Christians for service—will want the work to continue beyond their own involvement.

It is also important to note that succession does not usually take place at the last moment. Few effective plans are launched at the deathbed of an outgoing minister. In all the biblical examples cited above, considerable time (often years) was invested in training successors for their roles before the handover occurred. They were tested, refined, and equipped by the Spirit of God for the tasks ahead, ensuring that when the time came, they could function successfully without feeling overwhelmed.

By 2002, the sixth edition of *Operation World* was in circulation. However, the world was markedly different from even a year earlier due to the impact of 9/11. I was 64 years old, and although I was in good health with a sharp and active mind and body, Paul's exhortation to Timothy continued to resound in my heart.

In his first letter to Timothy, Paul warned: "Do not be hasty in the laying on of hands, and do not share in the sins of others. Keep yourself pure" (1 Tim 5:22). Paul was showing that discipling successors is a lengthy process fraught with dangers. It is not enough for a person to possess the right abilities and qualifications; the process must include rigorous attention to the potential successor's spiritual life and personal purity, as well as the discipler's own. If these aspects are neglected, the succession will surely fail, and there will not be a "fourth generation." One only needs to observe the numerous failures among prominent Christian leaders due to their narcissism, desire for control, moral failures, and unwillingness to prepare a succession plan.

At that time, I had four widely different areas of ministry responsibility, and I was actively seeking to hand over each of these to reliable people. My *WEC leadership role* had begun in 1986 when Jill and I served as deputy leaders to Dieter and Renate Kuhl. Evan and Jenny Davies later joined our team and took over my position, although I remained an integral part of the leadership team in a mentoring role. Robyn and I decided to move from our small home in Hillingdon, as we didn't want to interfere with the ministry of our successors at nearby Bulstrode. From 2002, we lived in north Cambridgeshire, about one hundred miles north of the WEC headquarters. Later, in 2010, WEC asked us to take on a new regional leadership role in Europe and South Africa for three years.

This change in roles and geography gave Robyn and me the space and time we needed to address and deal with our inner baggage. My issues stemmed from my teenage sense of rejection and a desire to please people, which I concealed with a cloak of excessive loyalty. In Robyn's case, parental deficiencies during her childhood left her feeling worthless. She found great help in her healing process through various godly people and by absorbing truth while completing a master's degree in spiritual formation. This journey led her to experience a joyous sense of her personal relationship with her Heavenly Father and her immense value to him.

Next, I desired to find a suitable replacement for my role as the *director of research at WEC*. Like my predecessor, Leslie Brierley, I struggled to find anyone within WEC to succeed me. I kept my eyes open for possibilities, and at one point, I approached a Brazilian brother, Ronaldo Lidorio, about taking on my role. He was a brilliant missionary and researcher and seemed ideal, but by then, his heart was focused on pioneering a new work among Amazon tribes. This situation highlighted the fact that finding a suitable successor can take time and is often a process of trial and error. Although he never became the director of research at WEC, Ronaldo later joined our international leadership team.

The only other individuals I considered suitable for the international research role were a couple who had pioneered a new work in Europe and were renowned for their research abilities. An approach was made, and the offer was accepted, so in 2002 Robyn and I prepared to step down from the position I had held for twenty-three years. Then, as they prepared to take over the research office, the couple sent letters indicating their intent to radically change the direction of the office and use it to train church planters. They even said they wanted to discard all our information files, which had been the bedrock of the office's output for more than two decades!

We pleaded with them not to make hasty decisions but to first come and acclimate before deciding the best way to function effectively. It was soon apparent that they were not a good fit for the role at all. Ultimately, they resigned from WEC altogether. I regard this as my most challenging proposed handover and a good reminder that much prayer and patience may be needed before such ill-fitting situations become apparent. We cannot see inside a person's heart or judge their motives, but the Lord can reveal what we need to know.

Third, *finding a successor to compile and author Operation World* was my greatest challenge. The book was my "baby," and some doubted I would ever be able to hand over that ministry. It was comfortable for me to be identified with a successful book, creating a temptation to hold on and not let go. My biggest difficulty, however, was finding someone with the gifts, vision, and courage to take on and "own" this responsibility. I often prayed that if such a person existed, the Lord would reveal him to us and make it clear.

A young Canadian, Jason Mandryk, joined us in 1995 as a two-year volunteer. He spent his first year at Bulstrode processing information and digitizing our extensive collection of papers. After watching Jason closely, I believed that here at last was someone who could possibly take over the Operation World ministry, so I did everything possible to prepare him. When he completed his WEC candidate orientation and returned in 1997, I began to gradually integrate Jason into the next edition of *Operation World* by asking him to write profiles of some of the smaller countries. He did very well, so I increased the number of countries assigned to him. Jason would jokingly tell people that he profiled the smaller countries like Monaco, while I tackled the larger ones like China and India. Regardless, as I mentioned in the previous chapter, I insisted that his name appear alongside mine on the cover of the 2001 edition.

Writing, like all ministry, is done best when it arises from our personal experiences with God. I told Jason that I believed he would benefit from some years in cross-cultural mission work to gain broad, practical experiences that might blossom into a greater credibility and maturity in his later ministry. I believed he needed to develop his people skills if he was to successfully lead a team. As an introvert, he also needed to learn how to be open and vulnerable with those around him. Subsequently, after completing the sixth edition, he spent two years on the ship *MV Doulos* before returning to his role with Operation World. After Jason returned to Bulstrode, we worked together on what would become the 7th edition, which was eventually published in 2011, with Molly Wall and others joining the team to assist Jason.

I had warned Jason that the 800-page length of the 2001 edition was the absolute limit, but their edition grew to over 1,000 pages. This size was too big for translation into most other languages, although a Korean edition was produced that required three volumes. Because of the size issue, an abbreviated version was produced in 2015, making it more manageable for translators and publishers. As a result, five additional language editions were produced. Ultimately, Operation World was co-led by Molly and Jason.

The events of 9/11 had far-reaching consequences in society and the mission world. The 2001 edition of *Operation World* included an extensive survey of mission agencies and their work around the globe. But after the "war on terror" began, every organization working in sensitive countries had to reassess and tighten their security, eliminating any publicity that might endanger lives or ministries. A decade later, when the 2011 edition was being prepared, Jason found that a comparable survey was impossible due to the security concerns of many mission organizations.

This edition also needed to include several new countries. Fragments of the old Yugoslavia had become independent states, South Sudan had been carved out of Sudan after a brutal civil war, and Afghanistan, Iraq, and several other countries required significant revisions. I contributed to these changes while working remotely from our home in Cambridgeshire.

Finally, *my role on the leadership team of the AD2000 and Beyond Movement* came to an end. In this case, no handover was necessary as the movement itself reached its conclusion and wrapped up in 2001 after having served its God-given purposes. My prayer was that this movement would be replaced by new initiatives that would be more influential and relevant to every part of the global church. One such network that emerged was the Movement for African National Initiatives, which formalized a 40-year history of African national movements. They affirmed God's powerful work across the continent and committed to accelerate the advance of the gospel through networking and collaboration. To me, this was a delight. God had called me to Africa, and the first *Operation World* was written to inspire Africans to pray for and obey the Great Commission. At that time, however, I couldn't imagine that dynamic African missionary movements, led by Africans, would be operating by the end of the century!

Now that I am in my 80s, many of my involvements in public ministry in recent years have been in Africa-related meetings, including video conferences during the COVID-19 lockdowns. My constant challenge to African leaders is to get ready, as Africa will be the only continent with a majority of young people by 2050, and inevitably, its very large and active church will play a leading role in missions as well as in the global church.

In summary, although I continue to promote the discipleship of all the world's peoples and plan to do so until my final breath, God has helped me hand over all my core ministry responsibilities to gifted and prepared younger leaders so that the work will not go to the grave with me. For any church or ministry leader reading this who has no succession plan, I encourage you to seek the Lord's will. Cry out to him and be prepared for an answer from heaven. The Lord Jesus is interested in the work of his kingdom and the redemption of mankind—he wasn't crucified to give people a comfortable lifelong career.

THE FUTURE OF THE GLOBAL CHURCH

One of my great ambitions was to write another book after the handover of *Operation World*. We had a superb and unique set of data and files that enabled us to give credible facts and figures about the wider world, religions, and above all, the Christian church. While serving in various leadership roles, I was too busy to make full use of this information to explore trends and their implications for the future. Now that I was free from the enormous pressure of working on new editions of *Operation World*, I had my opportunity!

I had developed little graphs from the 1986 edition of *Operation World* and its subsequent editions that projected religions and Christian statistics ahead to the year 2000, and in the 2001 edition, the projections extended to 2025. There was no space, however, to explain the trends or what they might imply for the future of countries, the church, and the progress of the gospel. My dream was to be "prophetic," in the sense that I could show what might be expected in the decades to come and how Christians could best prepare for the future.

The twentieth century saw massive changes in national politics and religious affiliations. Nevertheless, decadal rates of change have a momentum of their own. They are likely to continue and can be projected into the future, albeit with the caution that a radical adjustment could reverse any trend. For example, as I write this in 2025, the world has largely emerged from the catastrophic COVID-19 pandemic. But the impact of the Russia-Ukraine War and the dismantling of seventy years of globalization have created a perfect storm that could result in the demise of Western democracy as a viable governmental system, the collapse of both the Russian Federation and Communist China, and the end of the United Nations.

Today marks twenty-four years since the traumatic 9/11 attack, a pivotal moment in world and mission history. As a result of the attack, the West launched a series of misguided countermeasures that led to military interventions in Afghanistan, Iraq, Libya, and elsewhere. The fallout from these actions has contributed to the erosion of the democratic cause and the breakdown of two centuries of world order. Within the church, we have lost many of the freedoms we once relied on to evangelize the world.

The long process of writing *The Future of the Global Church* began in 2004 and took six years to complete. It was a fascinating journey to observe how, during the sixty years of writing *Operation World*, the church had become truly global. In 1960, almost the entire missionary workforce was Western, but by 2011, most workers came from nations that were once considered target mission fields. Missionaries now travel from every country to every country, and there is no political state in the world today without an Evangelical Christian presence.

In the book, I set a target date of AD 2050 for the trends I wanted to present to readers. This 40-year projection, or one "long" generation, allowed me to give smooth rates of growth and decline for the whole period. I also had a great desire to provide historical context by covering the progress of the church since the birth of the Lord Jesus Christ. Consequently, I included a two-page spread for each century, with the left-hand page mapping world empires and itemizing key events of that century, while the facing right-hand page showed the advances and declines of the Christian church, listing the important events in church history. I succeeded, but it took me over two years to compile and create the maps and diagrams for those forty-two pages!

Other sections of the book covered the world's six major religious systems, followed by the six major streams of Christianity. I detailed the main Christian movements of the past three hundred years, including a section exploring what I call the "Sixth Awakening." I then covered the movements of the last three hundred years born out of revival that transcend denominational distinctions—the Evangelicals and the Charismatics. I also covered every significant revival movement and the six great awakenings of the last three hundred years. The last Awakening, the Sixth (my own categorization), spans from the 1960s to the present. This current awakening has witnessed the astonishing growth of biblical Christianity in Africa since the 1960s, Latin America since the 1970s, East Asia since the 1980s, in the post-Communist world during the 1990s, and within the Muslim world in this millennium.

One part of *The Future of the Global Church* focused on the unevangelized world—first addressing the 246 countries and territories across the globe, and then the 16,000 people groups. For the first time, we were able to publish maps showing the homelands of the world's peoples and the extent of Christianization among them. Finally, I examined the missionary force and its growth over two hundred years. My goal was to equip other mobilizers, church leaders, missionaries, and researchers with the information and tools they need to promote world evangelization.

In a sense, my aim was to hand over my life's work to others as I prepared for the day when my service to God in this life would conclude.

I began working on the book from the home Robyn and I had established in the Cambridgeshire countryside. I no longer had a support team around me or help from an IT specialist to handle computer problems, so learning all these complexities was a major challenge. I often stared in despair at my screen or groped my way through manuals and internet searches for hours not knowing how to proceed. Robyn often asked me, "When are you going to start the writing?" I wondered if I had bitten off more than I could chew!

My literary agent, Pieter Kwant, did his best to encourage me, but I sensed that he wondered if this book would ever reach publication. To complicate matters, the whole publishing world was in turmoil due to the growth of the internet. Many readers now only wanted to access information that was downloadable to a device. As Pieter once said, "These days many people will only read information that is free and fits onto the screen of their cell phone or device!" Such a dramatic societal shift did not fit well with long technical books full of graphics.

The biggest challenge was finding a viable publisher. Although I had credibility due to the many editions of *Operation World*, this unique 256-page book proved to be only a partial success because of the turmoil in the publishing world. Several companies that had previously produced my books had gone bankrupt in the internet age. Finally, I signed a contract with the American publisher Authentic/Biblica, but right after printing, they decided to concentrate on publishing Bibles and cease all other book projects. *The Future of the Global Church* became a casualty of this new policy. Thankfully, InterVarsity Press stepped in and became the publisher. They arranged a whirlwind speaking tour for me across the United States in the spring of 2011. Many people came to the meetings, and we sold large quantities of the book, but this was almost the only proactive promotion it received.

In the end, I believe around 25,000 to 30,000 copies were printed, which was quite discouraging given the crucial subject matter. Gone were the heady days of the 1990s, when it might have sold ten or twenty times that amount. Ironically, for a book that examined trends, it got caught up in a trend itself—the collapse of the Christian publishing industry.

Global Mapping International approached me about the possibility of expanding the two-page sections on migration and urbanization into small books. Dean Merrill was commissioned to co-author these books with me, which were published in 2016. The first was titled *Serving God in Today's Cities*, and the second, *Serving God in a Migrant Crisis*. Shortly after this, GMI became another casualty of the internet and Amazon upheaval, and they closed their ministry. This was another setback for the ongoing impact of all three books. Although InterVarsity Press again came to the rescue and salvaged the latter two books, they were unable to continue the electronic or online versions. Consequently, the dreams I had of an updatable, massive online resource for the Christian community foundered. I am still waiting and hoping that a day will come when Christians with a heart for reaching the world will again have a way to access solid, in-depth information to guide and empower them.

The nineteenth and twentieth centuries were marked by increasing globalization and world evangelization, reaching every nation and thousands of people groups. However, that era is now grinding to a halt. The remainder of the twenty-first century is likely to be very different and will require new tools, fresh ministry strategies, and new recruits to complete the task Jesus entrusted to us.

Every book I have authored has been a huge struggle, marked by peaks and valleys. *The Future of the Global Church* was probably the most difficult book I have ever written, yet it is also the one that has pleased me most, even though sales were not all we had hoped for. It has now been thirteen years since we published the book, and it is helpful to reflect on what I got right and what I missed or was wrong about. The book identified nine global challenges and the future scenarios they would likely produce. Those assumptions have largely proven correct, including a section I wrote prior to COVID-19 that predicted the likelihood of a global pandemic.

The religious and Christian trends I forecast have generally been confirmed. The massive decline in the number of births in developed countries is slowing church growth and leading to a substantial decrease in membership across many denominations. The impact of extremist Islam on the Muslim world has been substantiated, as has the rise in the number of Muslims turning to Christ as a result.

I had assumed a more gradual shift in demographics and politics, but I did warn that unexpected events could change things significantly. For example, the COVID-19 pandemic and Russia's war on Ukraine have changed the world and disrupted the assumed continuance of globalization. Changes that might normally have taken twenty to thirty years have been compressed into just a few years. The Russian attack has greatly accelerated its population collapse due to emigration and war casualties, likely leading to the end of the Russian Federation as we know it.

Other significant divergences since the book's publication include a much quicker slowdown in population growth than anticipated. The enormous impact of this population collapse will cripple the economies of many countries. In 2022, news emerged that the Chinese population had 100 million fewer people than previously reported in earlier censuses, due to bureaucratic manipulation of birth statistics by officials seeking increased government grants. Further research in 2025 provided evidence of an even more catastrophic population decline in China, suggesting that the population may not be 1.4 billion, but rather around or below 500 million (see www.youtube.com/watch?v=UM57HhM8yV8).

I had expected the democratic surge following the end of the Cold War to lead more countries to choose this system. However, due to Western policy blunders, military interventions, and the rise of religious extremism and nationalism, democracy is in retreat, while autocrats, dictators, and warlords have multiplied.

I anticipated that almost the entire Muslim world would be engulfed in violence for a generation. This has happened in some countries, including Syria and Yemen, largely due to the emergence of ISIS as a violent would-be Islamic caliphate.

Finally, the massive expansion of evangelical Christianity in the latter part of the twentieth century has been considerably stunted and discredited by the politicization of Evangelicalism in the United States, Brazil, and other regions. This will inevitably have a negative impact on missions, while the collapse of institutional churches worldwide is underway, as the younger generation turns away from even the term "Evangelical."

We live in solemn and uncertain times. What I have shared may seem somewhat negative, but Christians must view the world through a lens of faith in God's sovereignty. He remains firmly seated on the throne of the universe and in complete control of the ultimate destiny of nations. Despite the chaotic events orchestrated by sinful individuals and the nations they lead, the timetable of the King of kings remains completely on schedule to fulfill his perfect will!

30

LIFE LESSONS

I have had a lifelong prayer that I would end my journey at the high point of my spiritual development. Too many of God's people—both in the Bible and in our communities—experience a decline in their spiritual walk later in life. Unfortunately, this has often been a pattern throughout church history. So I want to conclude my story with a summary of some of the most important lessons I have learned—and am still learning—during my six decades of serving the living God.

1. I thank God for the wonderful disciplers in my life—here are a few:
   - Peter Marshall, who first led me to Christ and discipled me at university.
   - Glyn Davies, who prepared me for missionary service in Bristol.
   - Hans von Staden, the leader of the Dorothea Mission, who entrusted me with huge tasks and pushed me beyond my imagined limits.
   - Norman Grubb, whose writings and later personal ministry helped me to really see who I am in Christ.
   - George Verwer, who saw the potential of the original *Operation World* and turned it into a global phenomenon.
   - Jill, my first wife, who introduced me to the Sabbath rest of God.

- Robyn, my second wife, who encouraged me to pursue ongoing transformation in my life.

2. I was a broken failure—only by completely surrendering myself to Jesus could he begin the process of repair.

3. I am created in God for a special purpose, and even my "imperfections" can be redemptive and enhance my ministry. Only a few years ago did I realize I had cognitive audio processing disorder (CAPD), impacting my ability to receive verbal messaging both in person and over the phone. Yet this challenge forced me to compensate with total concentration on tasks in hand—often frustrating others, injuring myself, and not noticing my surroundings. I believe it also made each *Operation World* a finishable project!

4. My life is like an onion with many layers—the layers of lies from the enemy that I believed. It takes a lifetime to expose and confront each lie, and I am still making these discoveries.

5. The hard knocks and pains of life, along with my wrong reactions, are God-given means of exposing particular lies and replacing them with the truth of his Word. Jesus promised in John 8:36 that if the Son sets you free, you will be free indeed. That freedom is progressively realized as we embrace his truth.

6. God answers prayer—in our needs, guidance, and in changing lives and situations. My last regular salary was when I was teaching in 1962, and I have never made a direct appeal for funds. I do not fully understand the Lord's financing arrangements, but he has seen us through. The only time I was totally destitute was in Africa during a period when I held onto a resentment.

7. I do not have to work for Christ, but rather work by him (John 6:57 KJV). For too long, I sought to work for the One who redeemed me, and I failed. I please him by my dependence on the One indwelling me and not on the time and effort I give.

8 There remains a Sabbath rest for the people of God (Heb 4:9). Consciously and daily surrendering myself to enter that rest is liberating. Resting in the abilities of Jesus, who is able to work through me, is liberation indeed.

9 Loyalty is a commendable trait, but not helpful if it leads to man-pleasing and an inability to sometimes say "no!" For too long, I said "yes" when I should have said "no," or took on tasks or responsibilities because I did not want to disappoint others.

10 Burnout in ministry is all too common and radically changed my life in 1983. I regret not taking a timely extended break between my time in Africa and my ministry based in the UK. I strongly advise those burning the candle at both ends to step back immediately. It is better to pull back from the brink of breakdown for several months than to spend a lifetime dealing with potential health problems. Keeping company with Jesus as one's first priority realigns all other commitments.

11 My assessment of my own personality, abilities, and ministry gifts is far lower than God's. He constantly pushes me into ministries and situations that challenge my comfort zone. He always provides the giftings and graces I need to fulfill his will for me (2 Cor 12:1–10).

12 The Holy Spirit is wonderful, and I need his filling daily. His graces are more important than his giftings, so my personal relationship with God is far more important than the public exercise of his giftings.

13 The one active verb in Matthew 28:18–19 is "to disciple." I went to Africa as a missionary evangelist—I was a biblical "apostle" (a sent one). Since then, I have been a teacher, pastoring missionary teams, but all of the fivefold ministry gifts in Ephesians 4:11 are subject to the command to disciple those for whom I am responsible. That means "alongsiding" them so they become like Jesus and are prepared for possible leadership. My aim is to have as many as possible who are fourth-generation disciplers, as stated in 2 Timothy 2:2.

31

A WORLD STILL TO WIN

In the last two decades, the number of Indian nationals engaged in pioneering cross-cultural outreach across the vast subcontinent has increased dramatically. Only eternity will reveal how much of this was due to my late colleague George Verwer's vision for India, which has become one of the largest missionary-sending countries in the world. William Carey's original vision from over two centuries ago is being fulfilled, with the gospel spreading all over India through fervent Indian disciples of Christ.

In 2015, at the age of 77, I traveled to northeast India to minister for five weeks in the states of Nagaland, Meghalaya, and Manipur—three of the seven northeastern states known as "The Seven Sisters of India." This region is populated by Tibeto-Burman-speaking tribes related to groups in South China, Myanmar, and other parts of Southeast Asia. Over the past century, the majority of people in northeast Indian border states have become Christians, often through great awakenings, people movements, and powerful revivals. The Christians are often well educated and highly motivated, but they dwell in mountainous areas with a poor communication infrastructure.

During my trip, I was hosted by Mizo, Garo, Khasi, and Naga Christians. There are now many large and thriving churches among each ethnic group, including one Naga Baptist denomination for each of the sixteen Naga language groups. It was thrilling to me to see how many communities had been transformed by the Spirit of God, and our meetings inspired some individuals to become missionaries in India and around the world.

In the city of Dimapur, an elderly man attended our evening meeting, clutching his well-worn copy of the 1986 edition of *Operation World*. It had been used constantly for nearly thirty years and was heavily marked and falling to pieces. I was deeply moved, and in that moment, all the pain and thousands of hours of effort to produce those books felt entirely worthwhile!

Later, in February 2020—when I was 81 years old—I made what is likely my final overseas ministry trip to Burkina Faso in West Africa. I left Britain as COVID-19 was escalating and returned just before lockdowns were imposed. The conference went well, and I experienced great freedom in my ministry and interactions with local workers. The terrible rise of Jihadist insurrections was already devastating Burkina Faso, resulting in one million people being displaced. We had a constant military guard throughout the conference, but fortunately, no incidents occurred. Regrettably, due to the violence, very few non-African missionaries now remain in the area along the southern edge of the vast Sahara Desert (known as the Sahel). The situation has become much worse since our visit, with the spread of violence and the withdrawal of UN troops and Western militaries.

The COVID-19 lockdowns brought a radical change in my ministry. I had traveled extensively for decades, but these lockdowns brought international travel to an abrupt end. In addition to the cancellation of flights and conferences, the huge increase in travel insurance costs due to my age has now made international travel unaffordable.

Instead of traveling, a new career has opened up with invitations to speak in dozens of online video conferences, especially for church and ministry leaders in Africa. Much of my teaching emphasized the need to look to the future in light of global cultural, economic, and spiritual changes accelerated by COVID-19 and war. As we move forward, we should not become despondent but remain deeply encouraged by the astonishing harvest that the Lord has brought into his kingdom in our generation, which he continues to gather in many parts of the world.

I have also continued to minister with WEC, for which I am grateful. The shift to WEC in 1980 was a turning point in my life, greatly expanding the reach of my books and ministry from southern Africa to a broader, global focus. The long-term headquarters at Bulstrode had been a superb base for multiple ministries and as a hub for WEC, but with the move of the international headquarters to Asia and the changes in culture and ministries, it was finally sold by WEC in 2023. Later that year, I completed my input into our latest WEC Candidate Orientation, which I expect will be my last contribution to it. Everything I shared was videotaped for posterity. During one session about WEC leaders, I realized that I am the only person still alive who has worked with every leader of the mission apart from the founder, C. T. Studd himself.

Robyn, meanwhile, has continued to enjoy her mentoring role, which is now mostly done remotely. She remains an introvert and enjoyed the two years of COVID-19 lockdowns, as she didn't have to attend large gatherings. As she mentioned in an email update to friends, "Church on a Sunday morning while I was sitting in my chair and enjoying my coffee was lovely!" After years of wanting to take up weaving, Robyn finally took the plunge and bought a table loom, which has been both a steep learning curve and a source of much satisfaction.

It has been a great blessing to see my children and grandchildren grow up and flourish into what God wants them to be, although there have been some extremely intense trials along the way. After Tim returned from serving on the Doulos in 1994, he met his life partner, Trina, at church, and they married two years later. He joined the Fire Service but was later diagnosed with multiple sclerosis, ultimately having to give up his promising career. Over the years, that horrible disease has gradually robbed him of almost all muscular movement, yet he maintains his strong faith and walk with Jesus. By 2024, Tim could only move his head and speak, although he now has an eye- and head-activated iPad.

Life has been brutally hard for Tim, Trina, and their two precious daughters, but he always has a smile and is quick to share a joke. He prays and witnesses to those he meets.

After a 28-year career in teaching and medicine, respectively, Peter and his wife, Julie, migrated to Australia, where they have lived for the past seven years, based in Grafton, New South Wales. They both became volunteer firefighters, and Peter was elected mayor of the large Clarence Valley region. Their three children are doing well as they pursue careers as teachers and accountants.

After their marriage, Ruth and Andy joined our organization as missionaries in Turkey. They spent seven years learning the language and then planted churches in the city of Antalya—two of my granddaughters were born in that ancient land. They later returned to the United Kingdom, where they now pastor a thriving church in Stockport near Manchester.

Although some friends wanted me to write only my biography and others wanted just the story of *Operation World*, in the end I have tried to combine both. It seems futile to separate my personal calling from the books that have been so closely linked with my name, millions of which, by God's providence, have been distributed throughout the world.

I am constantly humbled and encouraged when I hear about the impact *Operation World* has had on someone's life. While writing this chapter, I received a text message from a Malawian who, as a Bible school student in 1995, first learned about the needs of the nations through *Operation World*. A vision for world evangelization has gripped him ever since, and after serving as a missionary in India, he launched the inter-agency Malawi Evangelical Missionary Alliance in 2022. I praise God for this! His story has been multiplied hundreds of times around the world. For so many, *Operation World*, in its many languages, has been the spark that lit missionary fires.

As I near the final lap of my journey in this world with the Lord Jesus, I marvel at how he has used me in ways I never expected. Looking back, one of the most satisfying trends in my lifetime has been the shift of thinking in the mission world. When I started, missionary work was primarily "the West to the rest," but gradually I saw gifted leaders emerge from every culture who were better equipped to reach their own people in their own languages. While Westerners still have a vital role in the Great Commission, it is less about being frontline evangelists and more about coming alongside God's servants to help them fulfill the call of God on their lives.

After stepping down from my leadership role and handing over *Operation World*, my ministry has continued. I believe that everything I learned over six decades of ministry around the world has equipped me for further ministry. We face a more violent, poorer, and less stable future, with an aging global population and more prone to disasters, which will lead to further urbanization and an influx of refugees. Although Christians may have differing opinions about the origins of climate change, most agree that the climate is indeed changing. The effects are likely to increase migration from the most vulnerable areas, which will exacerbate many crises and increase tensions between nations.

These are the very things Jesus warned would happen when he spoke of wars, rumors of wars, famines, earthquakes, and persecutions. Crucially, the Lord also said, "And this gospel of the kingdom will be preached in the whole world as a testimony to all nations, and then the end will come" (Matt 24:14). The Lord taught that the chaos of the end times should not alarm us, for it must take place. I believe this means that those very hardships and sufferings will ultimately open hearts to the gospel.

An amazing example of this principle was seen in the tremendous revival in China that sprang out of the horrific sufferings during Mao's Cultural Revolution in the 1960s and 1970s. The spiritual void created by those tumultuous events prepared the way for the enormous turning to God that followed from 1980 to the present day.

A second example is the rise of violent Jihadist Islam, which has brought death and destruction to many parts of the world, with the vast majority of victims being Muslims themselves. This has led to a strong repugnance toward this form of Islam, with millions willing to renounce Islam and become followers of Jesus at the risk of their lives.

I have great hope and expectation that our precious Redeemer, Jesus Christ, will soon return to this earth, and the task of world evangelization will be completed. Until my final breath, I want to work toward that marvelous day when voices in heaven will loudly declare,

The kingdom of the world has become the kingdom of our Lord and of his Messiah, and he will reign for ever and ever."
(Rev 11:15)

Thank you for taking the time to read about my journey with God. One day, if you hear that I have left my earthly tent to be with the Lord, I hope you will be aware that anything good that may have come from my life has only been because of his great love and mercy.

Despite the deteriorating global conditions and our personal weaknesses, Christians must never retreat from engaging in global outreach until we have finished the task the Lord gave us in the Great Commission. He made it clear that the whole world must hear the good news so that they can know of God's offer of salvation.

We are not there yet, but we are much closer than many Christians realize.

May this book stir your heart and encourage you to be part of this great endeavor!

About the Authors

PATRICK JOHNSTONE is British and served God with the Dorothea Mission in Southern Africa for sixteen years as a missionary evangelist, discipler, and Bible translator. In Africa, he began compiling information to help people in Africa pray for the world. He then compiled six editions of *Operation World* between 1965 and 2001, with millions of copies distributed worldwide in nineteen languages. He and his first wife, Jill, were invited to serve for one year on the OM ship *MV Logos* and thereafter with WEC International as part of the leadership team in the UK, developing strategies to plant churches among the least reached peoples. Just before Jill's death in 1992, she completed a children's version of *Operation World*, titled *You Can Change the World* (now *Window on the World*), which was published in over twenty languages. Patrick has also served part-time leadership roles in the Lausanne and the AD2000 and Beyond Movements. He retired from active leadership roles in WEC in 2015 and lives with his US wife, Robyn, in Derby, England, while retaining his great passion for world evangelization and continuing to encourage and mentor mission leaders. He can be contacted by email at patrick@operationworld.org.

PAUL HATTAWAY is a native New Zealander and the founding director of Asia Harvest (www.asiaharvest.org), a non-denominational ministry that serves the church in Asia through various strategic initiatives, including the printing of millions of Bibles and supporting Asian missionaries among more than 1,200 unreached people groups. He is now working on many new full-color books profiling the peoples of Asia, starting with *Operation Myanmar* and a five-volume set of *Operation India books*, followed by *Operation Nepal, Laos, Vietnam*, and others. These can be accessed online via the Asia Harvest website. Paul can be reached at: office@asiaharvest.org.

visit us at missionbooks.org

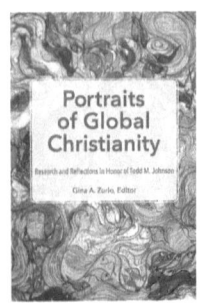

Portraits of Global Christianity: Research and Reflections in Honor of Todd M. Johnson
Gina A. Zurlo, Editor

This book is geared toward a general Christian audience and is written in an accessible style with attractive full-color charts, maps, and graphs to make quantitative data on Christianity and other religions come alive. The reflections and essays in this book in honor of Todd M. Johnson provide readers with concrete examples of how knowledge and experience of Christianity worldwide has fundamentally changed their worldviews, perspectives of the faith, and vocational callings.

People Vision: Reimagining Mission to Least Reached Peoples
Leonard N. Bartlotti, Editor

A mere fraction of global missionaries–less than 4 percent–are devoted to the unreached people groups (UPGs). This glaring disparity reveals a challenge in modern missiology. Over sixty authors reexamine our understanding of people group missiology from the lens of Scripture, reflection, conversation, prayer, and case studies from field workers and church/mission leaders. Readers are equipped with the tools to navigate and overcome the barriers hindering effective mission work among UPGs and envision innovative approaches.

Innovation in World Mission: A Framework for Transformational Thinking about the Future of World Mission
Derek T. Seipp

Innovation in World Mission explores the categories of mega-changes happening around us, and the impacts they are making, specifically in world mission. It explores how God created us in his image, to be creative and innovative–modern day children of Issachar who understand change and know how to respond. Real-life examples from ministries, non-profits, and businesses are used throughout to help understand how to put these tools into practice.

www.ingramcontent.com/pod-product-compliance
Lightning Source LLC
Chambersburg PA
CBHW060600080526
44585CB00013B/632